At 400 pounds (181 kg), this baby elephant has a way to go before she reaches her mother's seven tons (6 t).

A lioness with her two cubs in Masai
Mara National Reserve, Kenya

NATIONAL
GEOGRAPHIC
KiDS

THE ULTIMATE BOOK OF AFRICAN ANIMALS

YOUR GUIDE TO **ANIMALS** THAT **ROAR, RACE,** AND TOTALLY **RULE**

DERECK JOUBERT AND
BEVERLY JOUBERT

With Suzanne Zimbler

NATIONAL GEOGRAPHIC
Washington, D.C.

CONTENTS

African rock python

North African fire salamander

Hippopotamus

INTRODUCTION

DERECK AND BEVERLY JOUBERT ARE GLOBALLY RECOGNIZED, AWARD-WINNING FILMMAKERS, conservationists, and National Geographic explorers-in-residence based in Botswana. Their mission for more than 35 years has been the conservation of key wildlife species, with a focus on large predators.

The Jouberts have published 12 books, produced 36 films for National Geographic, and written half a dozen scientific papers as well as many articles for *National Geographic* magazine. Beverly is also an acclaimed photographer for National Geographic.

Their efforts have one aim: to save the wild places of Africa and to protect the creatures that depend on them.

Some of our happiest times are when we are close to elephants, learning from them. They are such sensitive creatures and extremely attentive to their family.

WE WILL NEVER FORGET OUR FIRST ENCOUNTERS WITH ONE OF AFRICA'S MOST MAJESTIC ANIMALS: THE LION.

For Dereck, it was the roar of the big cat that made a lasting impression. At just six years old, he found it terrifying and fascinating at the same time. What sort of mythological beast could emit a call so gut-wrenching that the car door rattled? Dereck felt it in his chest and in the dark outside. Everything else went silent, out of respect—or fear. Later, he saw the lions hunting. He had more questions than his parents could answer. That day changed his life.

Beverly had a similar experience when she and her family came across a lion pride living in a deserted house on a reserve. Beverly picked up the family camera to document what she saw. From that moment on, she never let anyone else use it. A photographer was born.

Our paths were destined to cross. Our journey into understanding, researching, filming, and photographing iconic African animals also seems to have been our destiny. We've now done just that for over 35 years. What captivates us is partly the knowledge that these creatures could turn and eat us in an instant. But there is so much more that draws us to this work.

Watch a gorilla or an elephant, and you will know that we are not alone. Look into the eyes of a lion or a leopard, and you get a sense that someone is in there—a brain thinking, an emotional being capable of feeling, a prehistoric creature that with the same sharp canines will tear away flesh and then gently lift up a day-old cub without harming it at all.

For us, what is fascinating about getting to know these animals is that, in many ways, they teach us who we are. They show us that there is a place for everything and everyone. They make this beautiful planet whole. Spending time with these creatures is magical, moving, and educational. We hope that you will discover the same in this ultimate guide.

—Beverly and Dereck Joubert

Lions, elephants, and doves compete for a water hole in the dry season in Chobe National Park, Botswana.

CHAPTER ONE

SPOTTED ON SAFARI

>>> **ARE YOU READY FOR THE TRIP OF A LIFETIME?** Then pack your camera and your khakis—we're going on safari! The word "safari" means "journey" in Swahili, a language spoken in eastern and southern Africa. Going on safari gives people the chance to observe animals in their natural habitat.

Africa's wildlife parks are home to thousands of spectacular species, but many safari-goers set out hoping for a glimpse of the large mammals for which the continent is famous. Most of these creatures cannot be seen in the wild anywhere else on the planet.

In this chapter, we'll take a close look at 11 extraordinary mammals. By the time our journey is over, you'll know what they eat, how they live, and what makes them unique. So what are you waiting for? Let's go!

ELEPHANTS

>>> EVERYTHING ABOUT AN ELEPHANT IS BIG. ITS TRUNK ALONE CAN WEIGH A STAGGERING 290 POUNDS (132 KG)! But an elephant is much more than its size. The massive mammal is also known for its top-notch memory, cooperative ways, and tenderness toward other elephants. When a member of a herd is injured or trapped, other elephants work together to help. The brainy beasts also seem to recognize other elephants they haven't seen in years. And bonds between mothers and their calves are so strong that even a nine-year-old spends much of its time by its mother's side.

Who's in the Herd

It's family first for elephants. A herd is typically made up of a mother, her calves, her adult daughters, and their calves. The oldest and largest female is the matriarch, and she leads the herd in all activities. When elephants face danger, they gather around their leader, keeping the little ones in the middle. If a herd becomes too big, the elephants split into smaller groups, but the new herds remain in close contact. A male stays with his mother until he is around 12 years old, and then leaves the herd to join up with other males or to go it alone.

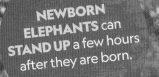

NEWBORN ELEPHANTS can STAND UP a few hours after they are born.

The Big Three

All elephants are enormous, but the savanna elephant is the largest of all. It is one of two elephant species found in Africa. The other is the forest elephant, which has rounder ears and straighter tusks than the savanna species. A third type of elephant lives in Asia. In this species, only males can grow tusks. That's not the case for African elephants, which can grow tusks whether they are male or female.

A baby Asian elephant eats food from its mother's mouth.

A HELPING TRUNK

An elephant's trunk is the ultimate tool. It is powerful enough to lift objects weighing 550 pounds (250 kg), yet it can also perform the most delicate of tasks, such as plucking a single berry from a tree. Here are six ways an elephant uses its trunk to survive.

BREATHE IN: The trunk is a combination of the upper lip and nose, with nostrils located at the tip. An elephant does most of its breathing through its trunk rather than its mouth.

THE NOSE KNOWS: With more scent receptors than any other mammal, including dogs, elephants can sniff out plants from miles away.

TIME TO DINE: An elephant uses its trunk like a hand, gathering food to place into its mouth. It can tear grass from the ground and also pick leaves and fruit from the top of a tall tree.

WASH IT DOWN: A thirsty elephant drinks about 26 gallons (98 L) at a time by repeatedly sucking water into its trunk and then squirting it into its mouth.

COOL OFF: The trunk works like a built-in showerhead. After spraying its body down, an elephant often coats its skin in dust or mud for protection from bugs and the sun.

MEET AND GREET: When elephants meet up, they sometimes intertwine trunks. It's believed to be their way of shaking hands.

An African elephant tears leaves off a tree with its trunk.

ZEBRAS

A zebra's **TEETH KEEP GROWING** for its entire life.

Grevy's zebras

>>> **WHAT'S BLACK AND WHITE AND STRIPED ALL OVER?** A zebra, of course! This eye-catching animal is found only in Africa. It is part of the horse family, and like its relatives, the zebra has a unique digestive system that requires it to eat constantly. When it grazes with its head down, its eyes and ears may not be on alert, so it is a target for predators—but the zebra is a first-rate runner. Its strong, bony legs are built for speed and distance.

When it's not eating or moving, a zebra can often be found taking care of its striped coat. It will wait in line for a turn to rub its body and head against a rock or tree or to roll in a pile of dust. Both activities help remove dead skin and insects.

Zebras are social creatures that gather and travel in enormous herds. How they group themselves within a herd depends on their species. What else makes each of the three zebra species distinct? Read on!

Grevy's Zebra

HOW TO RECOGNIZE IT: The largest of the zebras, it has a long face and big, rounded ears. The stripes on its rear form a distinctive bull's-eye pattern.

WHERE IT'S FOUND: A Grevy's zebra can survive on less water than other zebras, so it lives in a drier habitat. There are only about 2,700 of this species left, and most are found in northern Kenya.

Mountain Zebra

HOW TO RECOGNIZE IT: Look for long ears and a small fold of loose skin, or dewlap, hanging from this zebra's neck. A mountain zebra also has three or four bold horizontal stripes on its hindquarters and a bit of orange-brown fur around its nose.

WHERE IT'S FOUND: It lives in hilly, rocky areas in southern and southwestern Africa.

Mountain zebras

A LONG WAY TO GO

What a hike! A group of plains zebras in Botswana migrates to a salt pan more than 300 miles (483 km) round-trip each year. Scientists were amazed in 2012 when they discovered the length of the journey. They also noticed that the zebras walked right past other similar areas on the way to their salt pan destination. Why do the animals skip these places in favor of a more distant end point? It could be that the zebras' ancestors followed the same path, and this group is continuing the well-trodden tradition.

Plains Zebra

HOW TO RECOGNIZE IT: A plains zebra has a shorter neck than other zebras. Striping patterns vary by subspecies and from one zebra to the next. For example, some plains zebras are completely covered in stripes, whereas others have plain white fur on the rear and legs.

WHERE IT'S FOUND: This zebra needs a lot of water. It lives in sub-Saharan grasslands and woodlands where there is enough to drink. Also called the common zebra, this species is by far the most widespread.

Plains zebras

RHINOS

>>> WITH POINTY HORNS, AN ENORMOUS HEAD, AND THICK FOLDS OF SKIN ON ITS BODY, A RHINO LOOKS AS IF IT HAS BEEN TRANSPORTED FROM PREHISTORIC TIMES. Indeed, the rhino is one of the longest surviving mammals on Earth. Tens of millions of years ago, there were many species of rhino, including one that was the largest land mammal of all time. Today, there are only five rhino species left in the world. Two of them—the white rhino and the black rhino—are found in Africa.

How did the rhino manage to survive when so many other prehistoric mammals went extinct? Its secret could be in its ability to eat plant material that other animals could not. Its digestive system can tackle plants that would poison other animals, and its massive molars can withstand a lifetime of chewing hard-to-eat plants. It also helps that these giant beasts have few natural predators. One of the rhinos' enemies are the humans who hunt the animals for their horns, which sell for high prices. Though rhinos have a past that dates back many millions of years, their future is uncertain.

Rhinoceros means "NOSE-HORN." Both of the African rhino species, as well as Asia's Sumatran rhino, have two horns. The other two rhino species, the Javan and greater one-horned rhinos, both found in Asia, have only one horn.

A few weeks old, a baby white rhino sniffs the air.

White rhino

A DAY IN THE LIFE

To maintain its bulky physique, a rhino must eat around the clock. It uses its muscular lips to gather greens, which it chews before swallowing. Rhinos take breaks throughout the day and night and are least active during the hottest hours, when they can be found wallowing in mud to cool off. Male rhinos patrol their territories on their own, but females are often seen in pairs or groups—or with a little calf, which stays by its mother's side at all times.

WHICH RHINO?

Both black rhinos and white rhinos have gray skin. So, how did they get their names? It's said that the Afrikaans word for wide—as in "a rhino's wide mouth"—was misinterpreted as "white," and it stuck. The other species was perhaps called "black" to distinguish it from the white rhino. White rhinos are nearly twice as large as black rhinos. How else do they differ?

White Rhino	Black Rhino
The rhino's wide, square mouth crops short grass.	A pointed upper lip works like a finger to grab twigs and leaves.
The rhino's long head is carried low on its neck, so its muzzle can comfortably reach the short grass on the ground.	The rhino's shorter head is carried high on its neck, so it can munch leaves and twigs.
When the rhino raises its head, there is a large hump behind its ears.	The rhino does not have a hump behind its ears.

HIPPOS

Hippos find the best grazing areas by **FOLLOWING TRAILS OF DROPPINGS** left by other hippos.

>>> IF YOUR IMAGE OF A HIPPO IS OF AN ANIMAL IN THE WATER, IT'S FOR GOOD REASON. HIPPOS SPEND MOST OF THEIR TIME SUBMERGED IN A LAKE OR RIVER. IT'S NOT JUST A MATTER OF PREFERENCE, BUT OF SURVIVAL. The animals lose moisture through their thin skin and can easily become dehydrated. Plus, they rely on their watery refuges to keep cool.

A hippo is built for life in the water. Its nose, ears, and eyes are on top of its head, so that even when the animal is mostly submerged, it can continue to breathe, and it can hear and see what's happening above the surface. When a hippo ducks its head into the water, its nostrils and ears automatically close to prevent water from getting in. At night, hippos leave their pools to spend a few hours on land gobbling grass. The animals will travel up to six miles (10 km) in search of food. Their stubby legs can carry them long distances and also reach galloping speeds of 18 miles an hour (30 km/h). Before sunrise, hippos return to the water, where they will spend the day digesting their food and communicating with other members of the herd with loud honks and grunts.

A hippo on alert

DANGER!

With a round body, wide muzzle, and wiggly ears, a hippo appears cute and gentle. But make no mistake. This enormous creature is more *Ahhh!* than *Aww!* The hippo is known for being grumpy and aggressive. A group of hippos, called a pod, is typically led by one large male. If another male challenges the top hippo, it's time for a showdown. Each animal opens its mouth to show off its massive teeth and make clear that it is not afraid of a fight. Then they smash their teeth together like a pair of antelope locking horns. A clash can last more than an hour and leave one or both animals badly injured. The fight is over when one hippo backs down. Mother hippos are also known for their willingness to go to battle with any creature that poses a threat to their young. A hippo's bad temper, combined with its powerful bite, can spell danger for whoever crosses its path, from crocodiles to humans. In fact, hippos are said to kill hundreds of people in Africa each year, making them the deadliest large animals on the continent.

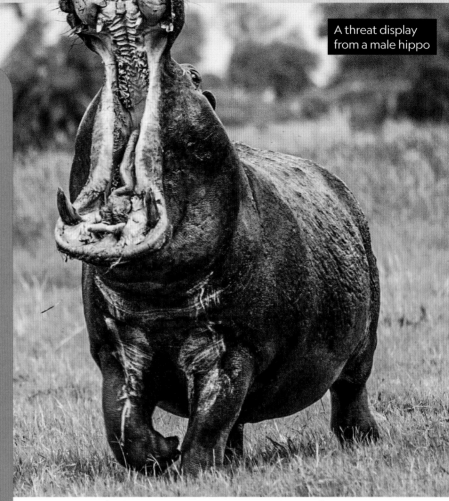

A threat display from a male hippo

MINI HIPPO

A pygmy hippo looks like a miniature version of the common hippo, but it is, in fact, a separate species—and different in key ways. Its eyes, ears, and nose don't protrude as much, and its head is smaller compared to the rest of its body. Pygmy hippos call the tropical forests of West Africa home, but they are so rare that it's a challenge to find them.

Pygmy hippopotamus

CREATURE BITES

Unlike deer antlers, which fall off and grow back each year, antelope horns **ARE NEVER SHED.**

A Grevy's zebra foal can **RUN LESS THAN AN HOUR AFTER IT IS BORN.**

Just as human babies suck their thumb, baby elephants suck their **TRUNK FOR COMFORT.**

Each gorilla has a **UNIQUE PATTERN OF WRINKLES** and marks around its nose. It's one way scientists studying the apes can tell who's who.

Male gorillas are the
LARGEST LIVING PRIMATES.

The tapir,
A PLANT-EATING MAMMAL WITH A FLEXIBLE SNOUT,
is among the rhino's closest living relatives.

Cheetahs are only active for about
12 PERCENT OF THE DAY.
The cats spend most of their time resting and conserving energy in preparation for their high-speed chases.

The word "hippopotamus" is Greek for
"RIVER HORSE,"
but hippos are not closely related to horses.

ANTELOPE

Common eland

>>> NO MATTER WHERE YOU GO IN AFRICA, AS LONG AS THERE IS SOME SORT OF PLANT LIFE, YOU ARE BOUND TO FIND AN ANTELOPE. There are more than 70 species on the continent, and each has evolved to survive in its environment. Antelope come in a variety of shapes and sizes. There's a tiny four-pound (1.8-kg) antelope and an enormous 2,000-pound (907-kg) one. Their coats can be white, brown, red, striped, or speckled. The animals also differ in how they move—there are sprinters, long-distance runners, and even high jumpers.

But all antelope species have a few features in common. The most obvious is their horns, which are made of bone and covered in a sheath of keratin, the same material found in fingernails. All male antelope have horns, and in about two-thirds of species, the females do, too. Like cattle, buffalo, and giraffes, antelope are ruminants—herbivores with a special digestive system that extracts as much nutrition as possible from plants. These animals regurgitate their food and rechew it, which is why they can often be seen moving their lower jaw from side to side. Want to know more about antelope? Get the facts on six standout species!

Heavyweight

There's nothing common about the common eland. Able to reach a weight of more than 2,000 pounds (907 kg), it's the biggest of all the antelope. It is also the slowest. Fortunately for the eland, it's large enough to stand up to most predators.

Klipspringer

All-Around Antelope

When it comes to antelope survival skills, impalas have it all. They are swift runners and impressive jumpers, able to soar 33 feet (10 m) in a single leap. And they can feed on both grass and leaves, ensuring that, high or low, they always have a meal.

Hop to It

To dodge predators, the klipspringer heads for the hills! The only antelope that makes its home on cliffs, it can jump from rock to rock with ease, always landing on the tips of its hooves.

Impala

Kudu

Holy Headgear!

The greater kudu has the longest horns of any antelope. At up to six feet (1.8 m) long, they are longer than a hockey stick! It takes six years for the corkscrew-shaped horns to complete two full turns.

In Plain Sight

Bushbucks live close to the forest so that they can hide among the trees. At night, they venture out onto open grasslands, where they eat and rest in a cloak of darkness.

Bushbuck

Dik-dik

Quick, Quick

The dik-dik is named for its distinctive alarm call. When it spots a predator, the antelope makes a "dik-dik" sound and runs in a zigzag to the nearest hiding spot.

BUFFALO

>>> **YOU WOULDN'T WANT TO FIND YOURSELF ON A BURLY BUFFALO'S BAD SIDE!** Buffalo are known for their aggressive nature, and their massive horns can do major damage. But these intimidating beasts also have a social side. They team up with one another to defend their herd's calves. They gather in giant herds of hundreds of animals or more. And they even lie on the ground with their bodies touching one another.

When they're not at rest, buffalo can often be found gulping grass. To sustain their size, they need to eat a lot. A buffalo uses its long tongue to bundle tall, coarse grass and then uses its wide muzzle to take big bites. It also eats some herbs and leaves. For a buffalo, scarfing food down quickly isn't rude—it's a survival skill!

A male Cape buffalo, or bull

Bison

BISON OR BUFFALO?

North America is home to a large grazing mammal that resembles an African buffalo. It looks similar enough that early explorers called it a buffalo. The name stuck, and people still use it today—even though, technically, this animal is a bison, not a buffalo.

How can you tell the difference between American bison and African buffalo? Bison have short, upturned horns, while buffalo have huge, curving horns. Bison also have a large hump at the shoulders, but buffalo do not.

The next time you hear the old folk song "Home on the Range," just imagine how it would sound if the North American mammals hadn't been misnamed from the start: *Oh, give me a home where the bison roam ...* It might not roll off the tongue, but it's correct!

A buffalo **COVERS ITSELF IN MUD TO KEEP COOL.** Later, the mud flakes off, taking along pesky insects that latched onto the buffalo's skin.

Herd of Cape buffalo

AN ANGRY MOB

Lions that go after young buffalo do so at their own risk. When a calf is in trouble, it bellows to rally the members of its herd. In response to a little one's distress call, a pack of angry buffalo will deliver a mob attack, chasing the lions into trees or even trampling the cats. By sticking together, buffalo can overcome even the fiercest of predators.

GIRAFFES

>>> **TALK ABOUT A TALL TALE!** When a baby giraffe is born, it drops onto the ground and stands up in as few as five minutes. At a height of six feet (1.8 m), the newborn is already taller than the average adult human. And that's just the beginning. A giraffe depends on its size for survival, so it needs to get tall as quickly as possible. It doubles its height within its first 12 months and reaches its full size by the time it is four years old. At up to 18 feet (5.5 m) tall, giraffes are too large for most predators to overpower. Their height allows them to feast on tasty leaves at the tops of trees; they can guzzle up to 75 pounds (34 kg) of leafy greens each day—a tall task, indeed!

LEAF-EATING MACHINE

A giraffe is designed for eating leafy greens. Check out four traits that make this animal a brilliant browser!

LONG NECK: Just like humans, giraffes have seven neck bones. But in giraffes, these bones are much longer. A giraffe's neck is about six feet (1.8 m) long and weighs a whopping 600 pounds (272 kg)!

Giraffes can gallop at up to **37 MILES AN HOUR** (60 km/h). But their legs are so long that even at top speed, the animals appear to be moving in slow motion.

Reticulated giraffes

TREMENDOUS TONGUE: At up to 20 inches (51 cm), a giraffe's tongue is longer than a bowling pin! A giraffe uses its nimble tongue to reach and pluck the juiciest leaves from its favorite trees while carefully avoiding spiky thorns.

SUN PROTECTION: The dark color of a giraffe's tongue is thought to guard against sunburn.

HEADS UP: The flexible joint between a giraffe's neck and skull allows the animal to tilt its head back to reach the highest leaves.

"Having spent years with this young leopard, from when she was 8 days old until she had her own cubs at 4 years old, we think we qualify as foster parents."

—Beverly and Dereck Joubert

LIONS

>>> WHEN IT COMES TO AFRICAN WILDLIFE, THE LION TRULY WEARS THE CROWN AS THE KING OF BEASTS. It is the largest and most powerful of the carnivores. Its mighty roar can be heard from as far as five miles (8 km) away. And though lions are known for hunting herbivores, such as antelope and zebras, they also prey on carnivores, including cheetahs and leopards. By teaming up, lions have even been known to take down elephants.

Lions live in family groups called prides. A typical pride might have two adult males, five to eight adult females, and their cubs. The females work together to do most of the hunting, and males spend their time patrolling and defending the group's territory from intruders. When members of a pride meet up, they greet each other warmly, rubbing their heads together—proof that even the fiercest of carnivores have a soft side.

A male lion

A lion mother and her cub play in the grass plains of Masai Mara in Kenya.

Oryx

Wildebeests

Zebras

Female lions, called lionesses, do the majority of the **HUNTING**—in between caring for their cubs!

A lion carries his catch to a sheltered area to eat.

Buffalo

THE LION'S SHARE

Lions work together on the hunt, but they compete for their share of the food. The cats fight for a place around an animal carcass, and top males take the largest portions for themselves. A lion can consume more than 75 pounds (34 kg) of meat at a single meal—and then not eat again for an entire week!

Giraffes

LEOPARDS

>>> **THE LEOPARD IS THE UNDERCOVER AGENT OF THE ANIMAL KINGDOM.** It lurks in the shadows, taking silent steps toward its prey. When it gets within a few yards, it pounces—and delivers a deadly bite. Then it carries its prey up a tree, where it can eat in peace, knowing that no other large predator shares its climbing skills. The cat is so agile and strong that it can even lug a heavy antelope high into the branches.

The leopard is a solitary animal that spends its days and nights alone, but there is one exception: Mothers stay with their cubs until the cubs are nearly two years old. Once the young leopards have been schooled in the ways of stealth, they go off on their own. But becoming a proficient hunter takes a while, so a newly independent leopard still visits its mom for a meal from time to time.

Just weeks old, this leopard cub is totally dependent on his mother.

Leopards are not picky eaters. They feast on nearly all types of animals, from tiny frogs to full-grown wildebeests. One study found that the leopards in Serengeti National Park eat 30 different kinds of prey. The park's lions, on the other hand, eat just 12. Here are a few of the many species leopards prey on.

A LEOPARD'S SPOTS

Invisibility cloak? Not quite. But a leopard's spotted coat might just be the closest thing. It is remarkably effective at helping the cat blend in with the background, whatever that background may be. All leopards have spots, but these spots look different depending on the cat's habitat. A leopard that lives in a rainforest, where there is plenty of shade, has a darker coat than a leopard that lives on a grassland, so it can blend in with the shadows. Since all leopards' spots resemble roses, the markings are called rosettes.

African leopard

Impala

Warthogs

Dik-diks

Guinea fowl

Squirrels

CHEETAHS

>>> IF YOU HAD TO PICK ONE FACT ABOUT THE CHEETAH, IT WOULD PROBABLY HAVE SOMETHING TO DO WITH THE CAT'S AMAZING RUNNING ABILITY. Indeed, when it comes to the question of which land animal is fastest, the cheetah wins, paws down. It relies on its record-setting speed to chase down prey. Unlike other cats, the cheetah usually hunts during the day. The cat does its best to get within 150 feet (46 m) of its potential prey, which is less than half the length of an American football field, and then quickly revs up to a sprint. If the cheetah succeeds in bringing down its target, it clamps its jaws down on the animal's throat, cutting off its air supply. Before digging in, the cat usually moves its meal to an area hidden by trees, but it still gets its food stolen by larger predators at least 10 percent of the time.

Learning to hunt starts early in a cheetah's life. Six weeks after her cubs are born, a mother takes them along when she hunts. At first, the cubs just watch. But when they are six months old, they are ready for some practice of their own. Their mother brings them small animals that are still alive and teaches them just where to bite the throat so that the prey won't escape. Practice leads to perfection, but becoming a top-notch hunter does take some time. Most cheetahs are still in training mode until they are well over a year old.

Cheetah cubs

Honey badger

A female cheetah on the chase

Gazelles

Impalas

Warthogs

Young zebras

Hares

GREAT PRETENDERS?

For its first few months of life, a cheetah cub's back is covered in a cape of long, gray fur. Some scientists think the fluffy fur is a trick that helps protect the cub. How? It makes a young cheetah look like a honey badger, a fierce and feisty carnivore. Predators familiar with honey badgers may think twice before going after a look-alike. On the other hand, the resemblance between honey badgers and young cheetahs could be just a coincidence. Take a look. What do you think?

GORILLAS

>>> **THERE WAS A TIME WHEN PEOPLE THOUGHT OF GORILLAS AS SOME OF THE MOST DANGEROUS AND TERRIFYING CREATURES IN THE JUNGLE.** But after decades of observing the apes in the wild, scientists now know that they are calm and peaceful much of the time. Found only in the dense rainforests of central and West Africa, gorillas live in a troop led by one adult male. The leader is easy to spot because, as the one mature male in the group, he is the only gorilla with a distinctive patch of silver hair on his back. Thus, he is called a silverback. The other group members are adult females and their offspring.

A gorilla troop is not a democracy. The silverback determines the schedule. He decides when the group will travel, when they will build nests to rest in, and when they will forage for leaves, shoots, and stems. If a young gorilla becomes too wild, all it takes is a frown or a grunt from the leader to put the troublemaker in line. But the silverback is more than a boss. He is also the defender of his troop. Silverbacks have been known to risk their lives for the group's protection, charging intruders while the others escape.

Gorillas usually **WALK ON FOUR LIMBS,** with some weight supported by the strong knuckles of their hands. But they can also get around on two feet—and sometimes do so to intimidate intruders.

Mountain gorilla babies play next to their mother.

JUST LIKE US

A young gorilla is a lot like a human baby. A newborn clings to its mom, but with time, the youngster begins to socialize and play. Groups are often seen rolling around on the ground and swinging from branches. When they don't get their way, the little apes throw enormous tantrums!

EAST VS. WEST

The eastern gorilla and western gorilla have much in common. Here's how they differ.

Eastern Gorilla

This gorilla has a black coat. Those that live in the mountains have longer, thicker hair on their arms to help them stay warm.

It spends most of its time on the ground.

Males weigh up to 460 pounds (209 kg).

A troop can have up to five adult females.

Eastern gorilla

Western Gorilla

Its coat is brownish gray.

It frequently climbs trees in search of fruit.

Males weigh up to 420 pounds (191 kg).

A troop rarely has more than three adult females.

Western gorilla

JOURNEY WITH THE JOUBERTS

THE LEOPARD THAT
CHANGED OUR LIVES

DRIVING IN BOTSWANA'S OKAVANGO DELTA EARLY ONE MORNING IN 2002, WE SPOTTED A LEOPARD AND DECIDED TO FOLLOW HER.

The leopard led us to her den, nestled in the thick branches of a fallen tree. As we watched her step inside, we could hardly believe our eyes: Her tiny cub lay hidden behind the branches and leaves. We stopped everything else we were doing and moved into the area to film the young leopard.

We decided to call her Legadema, which means "light from the sky" in Setswana, the most widely spoken language in Botswana. Early on, it was clear that Legadema saw us as just other forest dwellers and was not scared. She would poke her little head through the branches to watch us. Then, if there was a sudden noise, such as a baboon troop coming our way, she'd quickly retreat into the den she shared with her mother, or crawl under our car.

As Legadema grew, she ventured from the den to explore the forest on her own. We'd drive along behind her, observing and filming. Whenever we lost track of her, we'd try to follow her paw prints. Or we'd rely on the other animals in the forest to help us. When a leopard is near, other creatures—from monkeys and squirrels to the tiniest of birds—alert each other of the cat's presence. By following these squawks and chirps, we were able to find our way back to Legadema.

When she saw us sitting in our car, which is completely open, without doors or a roof, she'd sometimes sit nearby and stare at us with her beautiful amber eyes. On rare occasions, she'd walk over and tap Beverly's foot with her paw, then crawl under the car to Dereck's side and rest her face on his foot. Afterward, she'd return to whatever she'd been doing, carrying on as if such an affectionate greeting had never occurred.

It was a heartwarming relationship with a bridge of trust that bonded us. But at the same time, we were determined to be hands-off, knowing that if you touch a wild animal, you change it. We started training her not to cross this boundary.

Life Lessons

When Legadema was about a year old, she jumped into our car. We could have banged on the dashboard or shouted. But instead, Dereck turned on the heater. It blew hot air at her, which she didn't like, and she started to growl. A leaf that was caught in the vent made a rattling sound, and she didn't like that either. She left. The next couple times that she got into our car, we did the same thing. We found that we could maintain boundaries—and Legadema's trust—with caring and kindness rather than harshness.

After filming, we found out that in the four years we followed Legadema, 10,000 leopards had been killed legally. We were horrified, and we knew we needed to give wild cats a voice. That's when we started the Big Cats Initiative. Today, the program supports more than 150 projects in 27 countries. Our hope is that one day people will come to realize that Legadema and all big cats are far more precious than the skins on their backs.

CHAPTER TWO

BUILT TO SURVIVE

>>> **HOW DO ANIMALS LIVE WHERE THERE IS NO WATER TO DRINK?** How do carnivores eat when their meals are always on the run? What does it take for creatures to survive when fierce predators are trying to gobble them up? Nature has answered these questions by equipping species for survival in all sorts of circumstances.

There is a desert beetle that drinks by collecting moisture from the air. There is a cat that can accelerate faster than a car. And there is a lizard that detaches its own tail when it's being chased, and then later grows a new one. If you can think of a strategy for survival, it probably exists in the natural world. We've compiled some of the most extreme adaptations found in Africa's wildlife. You won't believe what some creatures can do!

AWESOME AFRICA

Rolling grasslands, scattered trees, and wide-open skies: This is the landscape that many people picture when they think of African animals. It's for good reason. Africa's savannas boast an amazing variety of wildlife, including many large mammals. But the continent's other ecosystems, from bone-dry deserts to lush rainforests, are also home to an incredible assortment of species. Take a look!

Sahara

In the Sahara, temperatures can swing from below freezing at night to scorching hot during the day. Some parts of this vast desert can go two years without a drop of rain. The animals that make their home here are built for survival in a harsh, dry environment.

THE ADDAX ANTELOPE CAN GET ALL THE WATER IT NEEDS FROM THE PLANTS IT EATS.

Ethiopian Highlands

Known as the Roof of Africa, this region boasts many of Africa's tallest mountains. Nimble creatures, such as the gelada monkey, are right at home on the highlands' craggy cliffs.

GELADA MONKEYS SLEEP ON STEEP CLIFFS IN THE ETHIOPIAN HIGHLANDS.

Sahel

This narrow band of land receives some rain during its short wet season, but the region is dry for much of the year. Animals here are constantly o■ the move, in search of water and plants.

Sahara

Sahel

Savanna

Ethiopian Highlands

Madagascar

For millions of years, animals evolved on the island of Madagascar, isolated from the rest of the world. Today, most of the creatures here cannot be found anywhere else.

THE FOSSA IS THE LARGEST CARNIVORE ON THE ISLAND OF MADAGASCAR.

Savanna

Here you will find many of Africa's most iconic animals, from elephants and giraffes to cheetahs and lions. Tall grasses grow during the rainy season, providing nourishment for herds of zebras, gazelles, and wildebeests. Where these grazers are found, predators lurk, too.

EACH YEAR, MORE THAN A MILLION WILDEBEESTS AND HUNDREDS OF THOUSANDS OF ZEBRAS AND GAZELLES MIGRATE THROUGH THE SERENGETI, A REGION OF THE AFRICAN SAVANNA.

Madagascar

Lake Victoria

Great Lakes

Rainforest

Savanna

Kalahari Desert

Namib Desert

WESTERN GORILLAS FREQUENTLY CLIMB TREES IN SEARCH OF FRUIT.

HIPPOS SPEND THEIR DAYS BASKING IN WATER AND THEIR NIGHTS GRAZING ON LAND.

IN THE RAINY SEASON, THOUSANDS OF FLAMINGOS VISIT SALT PANS IN THE KALAHARI!

Kalahari Desert

The Kalahari is no ordinary desert. In the rainy season, the mighty Okavango River spills into a delta here, forming marshes rich with wildlife. Long ago, there was even more water in the Kalahari. Where an enormous ancient lake dried up, a vast area of land now gleams with the salt and minerals left behind.

LIONS THAT LIVE IN THE NAMIB DESERT CAN GO WEEKS WITHOUT A SIP OF WATER.

Namib Desert

The Namib, a coastal desert, receives less than one inch (2.5 cm) of rain each year.

Rainforest

Africa's hot and humid rainforests are teeming with life, from chimpanzees and gorillas to parrots and forest elephants.

Great Lakes

Africa's great lakes are said to hold more than 25 percent of the world's unfrozen freshwater. Lake Victoria, Africa's largest, has hundreds of fish species. Many other creatures, including hippos and crocodiles, can be found in and around the lakes.

MASTERS OF DISGUISE

These creatures know how to hide in plain sight.

Male African swallowtail

Flying Undercover

Male African swallowtails mostly look the same, with wings that are pale yellow and black. But the females, which sport wings in several colors and patterns, can be hard to identify. Many look like inedible butterfly species, and that's no mistake. Flying undercover—as a butterfly that predators won't eat—helps keep these female swallowtails from getting swallowed up.

African stick mantis

Disappearing Act

Lounging on a tree trunk in broad daylight while surrounded by snakes and birds that want to eat you might not sound like a good idea. But the mossy leaf-tailed gecko can sleep in the sun for hours without being detected. Its bumpy, color-changing skin completely blends in with tree bark, speckled moss and all. The gecko's flat, leaf-shaped tail is also part of the vanishing act. But even its ability to blend into the background can't protect this unique lizard from being captured and sold in the international pet trade. Scientists say demand for the gecko and habitat loss in its native Madagascar are threatening the reptile's survival.

No Sticking Out

If it looks like a stick and acts like a stick, then it might just be ... a giant African stick mantis! Able to grow as long as a pencil, it is one of the largest mantises in the world. But when standing on a tree branch, it is virtually invisible. Even the little points on its head mimic spikes on a stick. The mantis waits patiently to ambush its prey. When an unsuspecting spider crawls within reach, the mantis grabs it with twig-like forearms and digs in.

Mossy leaf-tailed gecko

The Living Dead

Lake Malawi, in southeast Africa, is home to hundreds of fish species. One species has an unusual hunting strategy: playing dead. The Livingston's cichlid sinks to the lake bottom and lies on its side. There, its blotchy blue skin helps convince other fish that it is dead. When tiny scavengers swim down to investigate, the cichlid comes alive and gobbles them up.

Livingston's cichlid

WARNING: VENOMOUS!

You don't want to cross paths with these dangerous critters.

A Toxic Bite

The black mamba is Africa's deadliest snake. Able to slither at speeds of more than 12 miles an hour (19 km/h), it is one of the fastest snakes in the world. It is also very long. The average black mamba is about seven feet (2 m) long, but some grow to be twice that size!

The snake's most fearsome feature is its toxic bite. It uses its venom when hunting small mammals and birds, but it also relies on the powerful substance to defend itself. The black mamba is a shy, nervous snake that would rather slither away than attack, but when cornered, it will charge, biting repeatedly and delivering enough venom to kill an animal hundreds of times its own size.

The black mamba is actually not black, but rather gray or brown. The snake gets its name from the inky-black color inside its mouth, which it displays as a warning signal. There is an antivenom that can reverse the effects of the snake's bite, but the lifesaving remedy is not always available in rural areas where the snakes are found.

VENOMOUS OR POISONOUS?

North African fire salamander

Quick quiz: Is the black mamba a poisonous snake? You may be surprised to learn that the answer is no. Animals that deliver toxins by biting, stinging, or spitting are venomous, not poisonous. Poisonous animals, on the other hand, unload toxins when they are eaten. The North African fire salamander, for example, is poisonous. It has chemicals on its skin that make it toxic to eat. Bright colors, such as the salamander's yellow spots, are a telltale sign that an amphibian is poisonous. Predators often take note—and leave the colorful critters off the menu.

Just two drops of **BLACK MAMBA VENOM** can kill an adult human.

Stand Back!

Venom isn't always delivered by a bite or a sting. The Mozambique spitting cobra is one of several snakes that spit venom through holes in their fangs when threatened. Spitting cobras aim straight for the eyes, and do so with incredible accuracy. They are able to reach a target as far as eight feet (2.4 m) away. The result: a very painful sting and sometimes even blindness. It's a defense strategy that allows the cobra to keep its enemies at a distance.

Mozambique spitting cobra spits its venom.

A black mamba uses its tongue to smell.

A Lethal Sting

The deathstalker might sound like a villain in a comic book, but the name belongs to one of the most dangerous scorpions in the world. It is small for a scorpion—only 3.5 to 4.5 inches (9 to 11 cm) long. And its pincers are tiny and weak. So what makes this scorpion so threatening? The powerful venom in its tail. The deathstalker hides under a rock and catches its insect prey by surprise. Since its pincers aren't strong, it relies on a quick and deadly venomous sting to stop its dinner in its tracks.

Deathstalker scorpion

BORN TO RUN

Africa is home to some of the world's fastest land animals.

Cheetah running at full speed

A **CHEETAH'S CLAWS** never completely retract, so they are always ready to grip the ground, like a pair of soccer cleats.

Fast Cat

Run, run, as fast as you can ... but to escape a cheetah, you need another plan! Cheetahs are the fastest runners on Earth. No other land animal comes close to matching the wild cat's record-setting speed. While hunting, it can go from 0 to 70 miles an hour (113 km/h) in just three seconds—faster than a sports car accelerates. And cheetahs have been clocked reaching even higher speeds than that! But racing at top speeds takes a toll, and the cat can't sustain a sprint for long. A cheetah chase is over quickly—usually in less than a minute.

Big Bird

On the open plains where many ostriches live, there is nowhere for the enormous birds to hide. And they can't fly, either. So, when a predator comes along, what's an ostrich to do? Run! Ostriches are not only the world's biggest birds—they are also the fastest on their feet. Their powerful, long legs carry them at speeds of up to 45 miles an hour (72 km/h), covering 16 feet (5 m) in a single stride. An ostrich's wings help the bird keep its balance during sharp turns. Ostriches are fleet-footed almost from the start: Just a month after hatching, a chick can keep up with its parents.

Ostriches run in Kenya.

Let's Bounce

The springbok is one bouncy ante-lope. It is best known for its unique way of jumping, called pronking, in which it repeatedly lifts itself up to six feet (1.8 m) off the ground, and then lands on all fours. A springbok might start pronking to alert others to a predator nearby. But if a springbok is in immediate danger, it doesn't bounce—it bolts. Reaching speeds of 55 miles an hour (89 km/h), the ante-lope has been known to out-gallop some of its fastest predators. No wonder it has a spring in its step!

Springbok

ON YOUR MARK, GET SET, GO!

See how some of the fastest runners stack up.

Runner	Top Speed
Cheetah	70 miles an hour (113 km/h)
Springbok	55 miles an hour (89 km/h)
Thomson's gazelle	50 miles an hour (80 km/h)
Lion	50 miles an hour (80 km/h)
Wildebeest	50 miles an hour (80 km/h)
Ostrich	45 miles an hour (72 km/h)
Giraffe	37 miles an hour (60 km/h)
African buffalo	35 miles an hour (56 km/h)
Human	28 miles an hour (45 km/h)

Running Wild

Less than 10 minutes after it's born, a young wildebeest can run with its mother. It has no choice. To survive, it must be able to travel with the rest of the herd. Moving is what wildebeests are known for. More than one million of the large antelope migrate 1,800 miles (2,897 km) around the Serengeti each year as they follow the rains to greener grasslands. They can walk or run for hours on end. The antelope can also sprint, able to clock speeds of 50 miles an hour (80 km/h) when running from predators.

Wildebeest

CREATURE BITES

An African butterflyfish can **FLING ITSELF** out of the water to **ESCAPE DANGER.**

LONG EYELASHES
protect a camel's eyes from sand in the desert.

An African **BOMBARDIER BEETLE** defends itself by firing an explosive mix of **BOILING CHEMICALS** at its enemies.

Hippos can hold their breath for **FIVE MINUTES.**

An okapi uses its **EXTRA-LONG TONGUE** to wash its eyes and ears.

48

When threatened, a hairy frog can **CRACK ITS OWN TOE BONES** and push them through its skin to produce **SHARP CLAWS.**

A fennec fox **SHEDS EXCESS BODY HEAT** through the many blood vessels in its **GIANT EARS.**

A naked mole rat can survive **WITHOUT OXYGEN** for **18 MINUTES.**

When attacked, the **AFRICAN CRESTED PORCUPINE** raises its one-foot (0.3-m)-long quills into a crest so its body appears **LARGER AND MORE THREATENING.**

Secretary birds have **SUPER STRONG LEGS**—all the better to stomp their prey with!

TIME-OUT

To survive tough times, some animals assume a sleeplike state.

African bullfrog

No Rain? No Problem.

When the going gets tough, an African bullfrog gets going—underground, that is. The plump frog survives the dry season by burrowing deep into the soil and wrapping its body in a cocoon made of its old skin cells. The amphibian stays in a sleeplike state called estivation for months. As soon as the rains return, the frog breaks free from its homemade shelter, clambers up to the surface, and gets right to work, searching for food and a mate.

African bullfrogs are among the **LARGEST FROGS** in the world. When frightened or angry, they puff themselves up to look even bigger.

An African lungfish breathes air at the water's surface.

Fish Out of Water

The African lungfish has been around since long before the dinosaurs, and considering the fish's survival skills, it's no wonder how. For most fish, living without water is not an option. But a lungfish is fine even when its pond completely dries up. At the start of the dry season, the fish tunnels its long, eel-like body underground. Then its skin produces a mucus cloak for its body. In its protective pod, the lungfish falls into a sleep-like state that can last for months. Only when the dry season has ended and water soaks the fish does it emerge from its slumber.

Out of Sight

Madagascar's fat-tailed lemurs had everyone stumped. Each year, the squirrel-size primates vanish for seven months. For a long time, nobody knew where they went. But there was one important clue: The lemurs' disappearance coincided with the dry season, when food and water are hard to come by. Scientists wondered if the animals might be hibernating, surviving off the nutrients stored in their extra-chunky tails.

Researchers tagged 53 lemurs to track their location, and their assumption turned out to be correct. The lemurs were hibernating in tree hollows. The animals are no longer mysterious, but they are unique: No other primate is known to hibernate.

Fat-tailed lemur

READY, SET, REGENERATE!

These creatures have superhero healing powers.

Red-headed agama

Take Two

Somewhere in West Africa, a snake chomps down on the bright blue tail of a red-headed agama. But moments later, the lizard scurries away, leaving its twitching tail behind. Many lizards can drop their tail to escape predators, and a new tail will grow in later. For male red-headed agamas, the replacement tail offers an additional advantage: They tend to grow a club-shaped tail the second time around, ideal for whacking rival lizards!

A Tale of Two Tails

As its name suggests, the African fat-tailed gecko has a particularly plump tail—one that serves an important purpose. The reptile stores fat in its tail to help it survive periods when food is scarce. But valuable as its tail may be, the gecko does not hesitate to discard it in the midst of a high-speed chase. When the pudgy tail is released, it continues to flail about, distracting the predator while the gecko escapes. But that's not the end of the gecko's tail—a new one soon grows in.

African spiny mouse

An African spiny mouse can also **DETACH ITS OWN TAIL** to escape predators.

African fat-tailed gecko

Skin, Be Gone!

To many a hungry predator, the African spiny mouse might look like an easy target. But the small rodent has an escape strategy that makes it unique among mammals. To free itself from a predator's clutches, the spiny mouse can shed patches of its own skin—and make a run for it. The process sounds painful, but the spiny mouse recovers quickly, growing new skin in just three days.

Teeth Aplenty

The Nile crocodile's most powerful weapon is its super-powerful bite. Unlike mammals, crocodiles can chomp down with maximum force because doing so won't cause permanent damage. Why? Old teeth are constantly replaced with new ones. One study found that each tooth in a Nile crocodile's mouth may be replaced as many as 50 times over the course of the reptile's life.

Nile crocodile swallowing a fish

"This impala got up on its feet within eight minutes, a necessary step for these animals, which need to be able to run almost immediately."

—Beverly and Dereck Joubert

RECIPES FOR SUCCESS

Weird and wacky eating habits help these animals survive.

Dung beetles rolling a dung ball

An Appetite for Dung

An elephant can produce 300 pounds (136 kg) of poop a day. What happens to all that dung? Some of it gets hauled away by dung beetles—hardworking insects that burrow in dung, lay their eggs in it, and even eat it. In only 15 minutes, thousands of these beetles can find their way to a fresh pile.

The dung beetles that whisk away balls of animal poop are known as rollers. Working together, a male and female carve out a ball of dung and roll it away from the other beetles. They then bury their ball to nibble on later or to use as a place to lay eggs. When the beetle babies hatch, their first dung dish is ready and waiting.

Dung beetles **SHAPE DUNG INTO BALLS** so that it is easy to roll. They often try to steal each other's balls of dung.

Look Ma, No Hooves!

There are more than 70 species of antelope in Africa, but only one can stand up straight on its hind legs without so much as leaning on a branch. This agile antelope is called a gerenuk, which means "giraffe-necked" in Somali. With the help of its extended neck, a gerenuk standing on its hind legs can reach leaves and flowers more than 6.5 feet (2 m) off the ground. For other antelope of its size, that would be one tall order. But for the gerenuk, it's just another day of browsing in the bushes.

Gerenuk

Drinking Tears

On the island of Madagascar, a spotted moth lands on a sleeping bird. It has come to drink the bird's tears. The moth inserts its proboscis—a sucking mouthpart—between the bird's closed eyelids and sips moisture from the bird's eye for 30 minutes. The moth is not after the water, but rather the salt in the bird's tears.

Creepy, Crawly, and Crunchy

Aardwolves and hyenas are closely related. But when it comes to food, these two animals are worlds apart. While hyenas are known for gobbling up just about any prey they can get their paws on, aardwolves dine almost exclusively on termites. An aardwolf uses its sticky tongue to lap up as many as 200,000 of the protein-packed bugs each night. Bug appétit!

Pass the Salt

When elephants do not get enough salt from their food, they seek out other sources of sodium. One group of elephants in Kenya has visited underground caves in search of salt-rich rocks. Each elephant uses its trunk to feel its way through pitch-dark chambers and uses its tusks to dislodge stones from cave walls.

Aardwolf

WILD WEAPONS

These creatures have some serious headgear.

South African oryx

Long Horns

Long ago, people purchased the horns of the South African oryx because they thought that they were unicorn horns. It's easy to see why they were fooled. The horns have a spiral shape and can grow to be more than 3.3 feet (1 m) long. Oryx use the daggerlike horns to defend their territory and to protect themselves from predators. But the spectacular horns meant to help the large antelope also make them targets for trophy hunters.

Tiny Triceratops

Headgear isn't just for mammals. A male Jackson's chameleon sports thick horns, which it uses in duels with rival males. When two males face off, the reptiles turn bright green to show they are ready for a fight, and then they lock horns. Often, one backs down, changing to a darker color and fleeing the scene. But some battles turn bloody, with one chameleon piercing the other's body.

Male Jackson's chameleon

One of a Kind

Rhino horns are different from other animal horns. They are not made of bone. Instead, they consist almost entirely of keratin, the same material that makes up your fingernails. And while horns typically sit on top of an animal's head, a rhino's horns grow just above its nose. A rhinos uses its horns to defend territory, protect its calves, dig for roots, and more.

But their horns also put the rhinos in danger. In some places, rhino horn is ground up and used to make medicines, even though there is no scientific evidence these medicines work.

Rhinoceros

Tough Tusks

Two sets of tusks jut out from a warthog's mouth. The top set appears to curve upward into a smile. But make no mistake: The curve of these enormous teeth does not suggest a friendly invitation. Though the bottom tusks are shorter, they are razor sharp. When warthogs are cornered by predators, they fight back using these tusks.

Heads Up

The little hornlike knobs on top of a giraffe's head are called ossicones. At birth, its ossicones are made of soft cartilage. Over time, they ossify, or turn into bone. Having well-developed ossicones can help male giraffes during "necking" contests. A male will swing his neck to smack his head into the body of his rival. Ossicones add weight to a giraffe's head, allowing for heavier blows.

Giraffe

Warthog

SAFE IN THE SUN

These cool animals know how to beat the heat.

Namib desert beetle collecting water

Out of Thin Air

It hardly ever rains in the desert, but that doesn't stop the Namib desert beetle from getting a drink. When the fog rolls in, the little beetle stands on its head and lifts its wings to catch tiny droplets from the humid air. The water accumulates and then trickles down into the beetle's mouth.

No Sweat

An ancient myth held that hippos sweat blood. In fact, the oily red substance that oozes from a hippo's skin is neither sweat nor blood. Instead, it's a cool tool for survival. The fluid acts as a sunblock, filtering out UV rays. The substance also has germ-fighting properties to help guard against infection and heal the aggressive animal's many scratches and cuts.

Hippopotamus skin

Snake in the Sand

Blazing-hot sand? No problem. The Namib desert viper's sidewinding motion ensures that only two points of its body touch the hot ground at any one time as it zips through the desert at speeds of up to 18 miles an hour (30 km/h). With eyes on the top of its head, the viper can bury itself under the sand to stay cool and still keep watch for potential prey. When a lizard passes by, the vigilant viper is ready to pounce and deliver a venomous bite.

Namib desert viper

Addax

Color Changer

No other antelope is more adapted for life in the Sahara than the addax. It has wide hooves for walking in the sand. It gets all the water it needs from plants. And its fur color changes depending on the season. In winter, its fur is smoky gray, a color that absorbs heat. In summer, its coat turns white to reflect the sun's rays.

An Undercover Tail

Many small mammals that live in the desert are nocturnal, or active only at night. They spend the hottest hours of the day sleeping in the shade. But not the Cape ground squirrel. Instead, the rodent searches for food all day in the sweltering sun. When it needs to cool off, it simply uses its bushy tail as an umbrella for shade.

Cape ground squirrel

61

JOURNEY WITH THE JOUBERTS

SNAKY ENCOUNTERS

IF YOU'VE HEARD ABOUT THE MOST VENOMOUS SNAKES IN AFRICA, SUCH AS THE BLACK MAMBA OR THE BOOMSLANG, YOU MAY BE WONDERING IF WE'VE EVER COME ACROSS THEM. The truth is that our interactions with snakes over the years have been few and far between. Most of the snakes we've seen have been in a rush to get away from us. But of course, a snake will defend itself if it feels cornered—even if we didn't intend to corner it. Dereck has endured a few snake bites. One came from the infamous boomslang.

One late afternoon, not far from our tent, Dereck was working to connect a wire around a tree and suddenly felt a stabbing pain in his hand. At first, he thought that perhaps a wasp had stung him or that maybe a thorn had pricked his skin. We immediately started treating him with antihistamines. But as the hours went by, he became woozy and his heartbeat picked up. We realized we needed to know what exactly had bitten Dereck.

At 5 a.m., he was feeling worse. He went out to investigate and found the snake curled up behind that same tree. Based on its small size and its large, bright eyes, we thought it might be a boomslang. We sent out photos to confirm the species and soon learned that our hunch was correct. A nurse was rushed to our camp to medicate Dereck.

Once 12 hours had passed, we knew Dereck was safe, at least for the time being. But we were also aware that a boomslang bite can cause deadly complications several days after it's delivered. Dereck reached out to experts, and one, Richard Leakey, wrote: "Yes, it is a boomslang. If you are still alive, good for you. You will probably die in ten days." So, we took a break from filming to get Dereck to a hospital. With proper treatment, he returned to full health—and we soon returned to the bush to continue our project.

An Unforgettable Scene

Though few snakes have approached us, we have seen them interact with other creatures over the years. We'll never forget one incident with a python. As we approached our tent one night, we noticed a mysterious flash of movement in the dark. We stepped inside, wondering what might be lurking nearby.

Moments later, we heard a piercing scream. Flashlights in hand, we ran back out, and it was immediately clear what had been moving in the dark: an enormous, slithering python. We also discovered the source of the noise. Just beside our tent was a family of impalas, which are small antelope. The python had grabbed the leg of a foal and was wrapping its body around the little antelope. Pythons are not venomous, but they squeeze their prey until it's no longer breathing.

For a moment, we stood there, shocked. But then we ran to fetch our cameras. As we had done so many times before, we set aside our own emotions to focus on filming the extraordinary interaction unfolding before our eyes.

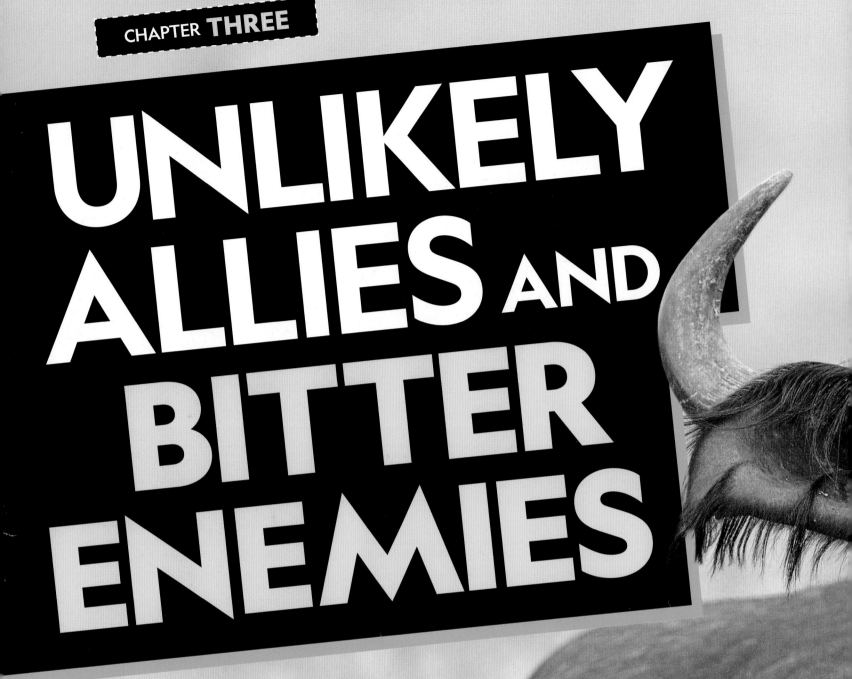

CHAPTER THREE

UNLIKELY ALLIES AND BITTER ENEMIES

>>> **WHEN WE THINK ABOUT HOW DIFFERENT SPECIES INTERACT WITH ONE ANOTHER, WE OFTEN FOCUS ON WHO HUNTS WHOM.** But there are relationships in the animal kingdom that go beyond predator and prey.

On the one hand, there are rivals, such as lions and hyenas. Each of these carnivores tries to take the other's food. But their bad blood is about more than competition—their vicious interactions seem to suggest that they deeply dislike each other. On the other hand, there are species that help each other. Oxpeckers often perch themselves on the bodies of large herbivores, such as rhinos and African buffalo. The birds remove pests from the mammals' skin—and get a protein-rich meal in return.

Are the lion and hyena truly enemies? Is the relationship between an oxpecker and a rhino a real friendship? You be the judge.

A yellow-billed oxpecker sits on an African buffalo.

THE SNAKE AND THE MONGOOSE

A puny-looking predator stands up to the world's most dangerous serpents.

>>> **A COBRA HAS LITTLE TO FEAR IN THE WILD.** Its powerful venom is reason enough for most creatures to keep their distance. But one little mammal has long been known as a formidable opponent of the cobra—and other venomous snakes. That mammal is the mongoose.

The mongoose's ability to take down deadly serpents has been noted for centuries. Its superquick reflexes and a powerful bite certainly help. But scientists suspected the mongoose had another trick up its sleeve. Time and again, mongooses were seen surviving what should have been deadly snake bites.

In the 1990s, a team of researchers got to the bottom of the mystery. They confirmed their suspicion: A mongoose is born with its own line of defense against snake venom. Normally, toxins in snake venom attach to receptors on a victim's muscle cells, paralyzing the victim. But a mongoose has special receptors that resist these toxins. Instead of binding, the toxins bounce off. This venom-defying superpower explains the mongoose's ability to stand up to its frightening foe.

A mongoose and a cobra face off.

Pink pigeon

MONGOOSE MISTAKE

In the late 19th and early 20th centuries, mongooses were brought to numerous islands around the world. The hope was that the plucky predators would combat rodents and snakes in these areas. But introducing mongooses to ecosystems where they didn't belong caused big problems. On the African island of Mauritius, for example, mongooses and other non-native species preyed on rare pink pigeons. The birds were also impacted by habitat destruction. By 1991, as few as nine pink pigeons remained. Conservation efforts have since brought the birds back from the brink. As of 2018, 470 wild pink pigeons could be found flying around Mauritius.

HUNTING HELPERS:
THE GELADA AND THE WOLF

These monkeys never cry wolf.

>>> GELADA MONKEYS LIVE IN THE ETHIOPIAN HIGHLANDS, where they spend their days munching on tasty grass and their nights sleeping on the edge of steep cliffs. Their mountainous habitat and their appetite for grass are unique for a monkey species, but even more unique is their willingness to hang out with predatory wolves.

On one rugged mountain plateau, Ethiopian wolves regularly join gelada monkeys grazing in the fields. Instead of running away or attempting to chase off the wolves, the baboon-size monkeys simply go about their business. They seem to know that the wolves have not come to prey on them. Instead, the carnivores are there to forage for a smaller snack: underground rats. And when it comes to snagging tasty rodents, the geladas are a great help to the wolves. When the monkeys graze, they disturb the rats in their dens, making it easier for the wolves to catch them.

When the wolves forage without any geladas nearby, they nab a rodent only 25 percent of the time. But when they hunt near their grazing monkey pals, their success rate climbs to 67 percent. That's some good monkey business!

Gelada monkey

68

Geladas spend most of their time sitting down, **PLUCKING BLADES OF GRASS.** They have fatty pads on their bottoms to help them stay comfortable.

WOLVES
ON THE BRINK

The Ethiopian wolf is one of Africa's most endangered animals. Plagued by habitat loss and rabies outbreaks, the wolf's population has been shrinking for years. In 2014, scientists conducted tests to find out how they could get the wolves to swallow rabies vaccines. They hid the medicine in different types of bait, including dead rats, intestines, and goat meat, which turned out to be the wolves' favorite. Using what they learned, scientists are now working to give the rare wolves a population boost.

Ethiopian wolf with a captured rat

THE OXPECKER BIRD

Oxpeckers help rid large mammals of pesky ticks, but the birds also have a taste for blood.

OXPECKER NESTS are lined with grass, dry dung, and hair that the birds pluck from their mammal pals.

Yellow-billed oxpecker on an African buffalo

Red- and yellow-billed oxpeckers perch atop a female hippo while her baby basks in the winter sun.

›››FOR A TALL GIRAFFE OR A STOCKY HIPPO, REMOVING TICKS CAN BE QUITE A CHALLENGE. Some of the blood-sucking pests can be flicked away, but what about the ones that are out of reach? Fortunately for many large mammals on the African savanna, birds known as oxpeckers are there to help.

Oxpeckers can often be found perched on top of their giant hosts, using their beaks to pluck off ticks, flies, and maggots. The birds get a protein-rich meal. The mammals get rid of irritating, disease-carrying parasites. It seems to be a win-win situation—a perfect example of mutualistic behavior, which is different species helping each other.

But bugs aren't all that the birds gobble up from their hosts. Oxpeckers also feed on blood from the mammals' wounds. By doing so, the birds might be helping to keep the mammals' cuts clean. On the other hand, they could be interfering with the healing process.

Still, oxpeckers probably do more good than harm. In addition to picking off pests, the birds hiss when they are alarmed, alerting the beasts to possible danger. No wonder so many large mammals stand by—and stand still for—these feathered friends!

"This African rock python shows his beauty as he slowly slithers over a log."
—Beverly and Dereck Joubert

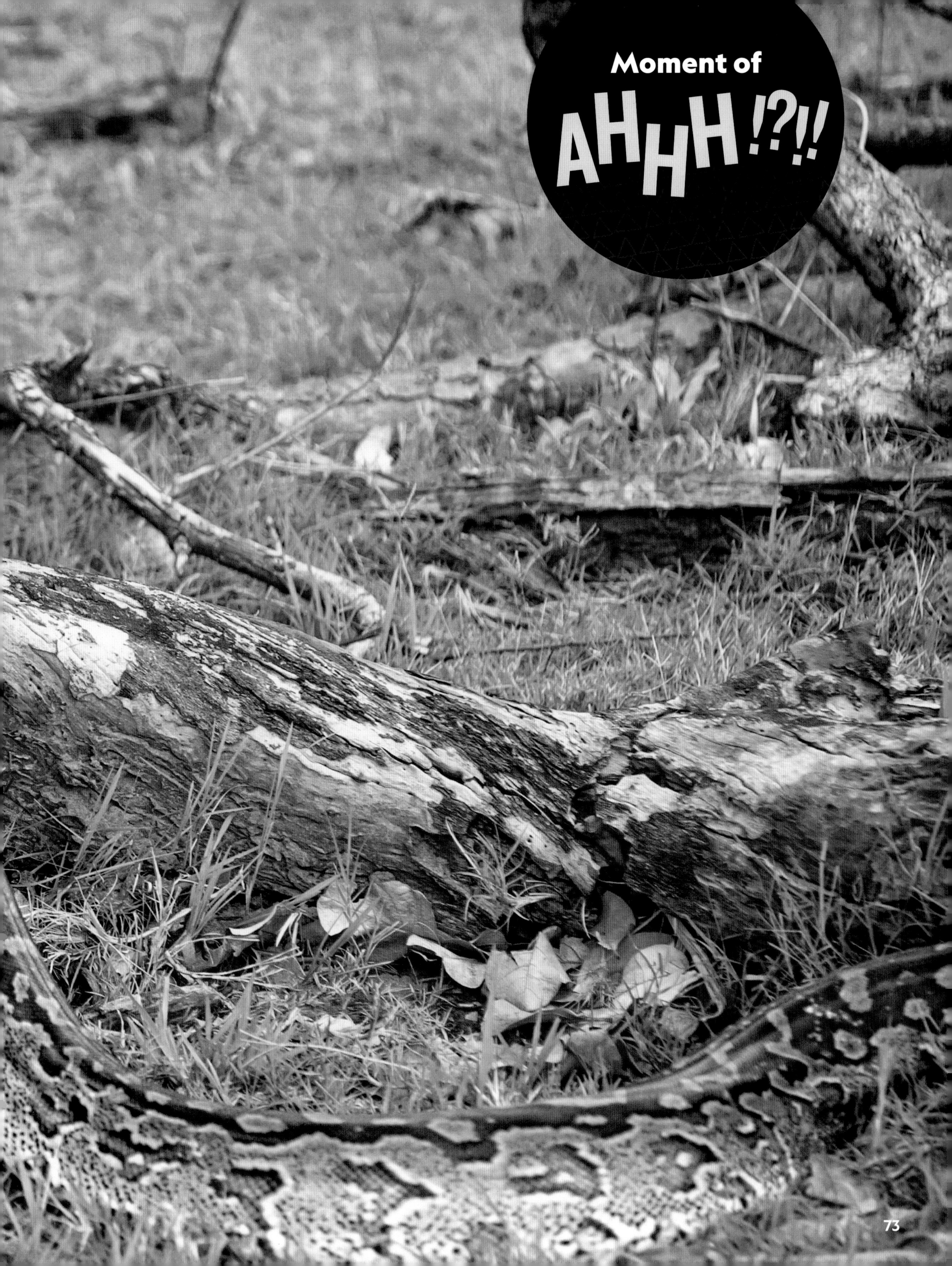
Moment of
AHHH !?!!

CREATURE BITES

The snake eagle is named for its **FAVORITE MEAL—** which it often gobbles **HEAD FIRST!**

Vervet monkeys have **SPECIAL ALARM CALLS** for certain predators, including **LEOPARDS, EAGLES,** and **SNAKES.**

Zebras and wildebeests are **GRAZING PARTNERS.** Zebras eat the tougher grass, making it easier for wildebeests to reach the soft, juicy grass they prefer.

CHEWED-UP LION BONES have been found in prehistoric hyena dens, suggesting that the carnivores have been enemies for **THOUSANDS OF YEARS.**

Ocean sunfish rely on seabirds to
PICK PARASITES OFF THEIR SKIN.
The fish swim to the water's surface
and lie waiting for the birds to begin their cleaning job.

A mini antelope called a Guenther's dik-dik
EAVESDROPS
on the alarm calls of go-away birds that sit high in the trees and
WATCH FOR PREDATORS.

Mongooses have been known to
GROOM WARTHOGS,
devouring ticks from the pigs' fur.

The fan-fingered gecko can
survive the equivalent of
100 STINGS'
worth of
**SCORPION
VENOM.**

Hyenas and warthogs have
been known to
**PEACEFULLY
SHARE
DENS.**
Hyenas use the lodgings
by day, and warthogs take
over at night.

ULTIMATE MATCHUPS

Fur flies when these fierce creatures face off.

LEOPARD VS. BABOON

Leopards hunt baboons from time to time, though they prefer other types of prey. While the cat is larger and more powerful than its primate opponents, it hunts alone, and baboons team up to retaliate.

KILLER CLIMBERS: AT NIGHT, LEOPARDS CLIMB TALL TREES TO PREY ON SLEEPING BABOONS. WITH A SWIFT BITE TO THE NECK, THE HUNT IS OVER.

LION VS. ELEPHANT

DEFENSIVE RING: ELEPHANTS PROTECT THEIR CALVES BY SURROUNDING THEM. ADULTS FACE OUTWARD, DISPLAYING THEIR TUSKS, TO PREVENT LIONS FROM ATTACKING.

Lions are the only predators powerful enough to take down an adult elephant. It takes several lionesses or two male lions to hunt the largest animal on Earth.

AMBUSH: TO AVOID AN ELEPHANT'S TUSKS, LIONS ATTACK FROM BEHIND. THE CATS TEND TO TARGET THE SMALLER FEMALE ELEPHANTS AND CALVES.

MEGA MONKEYS: IN THE LIGHT OF DAY, A MOB OF SHARP-TOOTHED BABOONS CAN SCARE OFF A LEOPARD.

Crocs and hippos are often found hanging out in the same rivers and lakes. Most of the time, they ignore each other. But if a croc is caught trying to prey on a hippo calf, the reptile better watch out. Hippo jaws can bite a crocodile in two!

CROC VS. HIPPO

TEETH OF TERROR: A HIPPO'S LOWER CANINES ARE RAZOR-SHARP AND CAN GROW TO BE 20 INCHES (51 CM) LONG.

SCAREDY-CAT: A CHEETAH'S TEMPERATURE RISES AFTER THE CAT MAKES A KILL. WHY? SCIENTISTS THINK THE CHEETAH IS STRESSED THAT OTHER PREDATORS MIGHT STEAL ITS FOOD.

A POWERFUL BITE: TO TEAR APART ITS PREY, A CROCODILE CHOMPS DOWN AND THEN TURNS ITS BODY IN THE WATER WITHOUT LETTING GO.

PACK MENTALITY: AFRICAN WILD DOGS HUNT IN PACKS, SUCCESSFULLY TAKING DOWN MOST OF THE PREY THEY PURSUE.

CHEETAH VS. AFRICAN WILD DOG

A cheetah is built for speed, not for fighting. If a pack of African wild dogs challenges a cheetah for its meal, the cat will probably run off in fear.

THE RED COLOBUS AND THE DIANA MONKEY

Two monkey species team up in the rainforest.

Red colobus monkey

>>> IN THE DENSE RAINFOREST OF THE IVORY COAST IN WEST AFRICA, THE RED COLOBUS IS A FAVORITE MEAL OF HUNGRY CHIMPANZEES. During the rainy season, when chimps are on the hunt, red colobus monkeys seek out their friends the Diana monkeys. Dianas are known for their super-loud alarm calls. When chimps are nearby, the Dianas make a terrible racket, ensuring that everyone knows to watch out. Then all the little monkeys scamper up to high branches that are too thin to hold the chimps' weight.

Even though the red colobus monkeys appear to get the most out of the arrangement, the Dianas are thought to benefit, too. To escape the eagles that prey on both types of monkeys, there is safety in numbers. By joining forces, red colobus and Diana monkeys protect themselves from predators in the sky and on the ground.

Diana monkey

Chimp holding prey

CHIMPS
ON THE HUNT

Chimpanzees are often seen eating fruit, termites, and leaves. But the apes also have a taste for meat and are known to use different hunting techniques, depending on where they live. In the rainforests of the Ivory Coast, male chimps hunt in groups, chasing their prey. The chimps feast on monkeys, pigs, and small antelope. In Senegal, where prey is harder to come by, female chimps hunt, too. Sometimes, they use broken branches to poke at galagos, or bush babies, hiding in trees. When one of the tiny primates comes out of hiding, the chimp pounces—making a meal of its squirrel-size prey.

SCARY
SOUNDS

How do we know that the monkeys team up primarily for protection from chimps? Scientists tested the theory by broadcasting the sounds of different predators over loudspeakers while watching how the monkeys responded. When the researchers played a recording of chimps hooting, the red colobus monkeys rushed to join forces with the Dianas. But recordings of leopards and a loud machine both failed to trigger the same response.

For Diana monkeys, the **MOTHER-DAUGHTER BOND IS STRONG.** Females stay with their mothers as long as they are both alive.

79

AN ANCIENT RIVALRY

THE WAR BETWEEN LIONS AND HYENAS HAS GONE ON FOR THOUSANDS OF YEARS. But since most of their battles are waged in the dark, record of their rivalry remained in the dark, too. In the 1980s, we set out to change that by filming lions and hyenas around the clock. What we learned was surprising, fascinating, and, at times, chilling.

Though hyenas are self-sufficient hunters, they are also known to trail other predators, hoping to seize someone else's catch. Sometimes, hyenas steal prey from lions. One night, we watched as a group of eight female lions hunted for hours without success. They must have been exhausted, but they kept going. Finally, they caught two tsessebe, which are large antelope. A few of the lions ran to fetch their cubs. They wanted the little ones to eat.

But just as the lions returned with their cubs, a massive clan of hyenas descended upon them, rushing in like wrecking balls. It was hair-raising to witness, knowing the hyenas could easily snatch the cubs. But the lions—with their cubs in tow—managed to escape into the branches of some nearby trees. From there, they watched as the hyenas lapped up their meal. The lions went hungry, but at least they all survived.

Of course, hyenas don't always come out on top. We will never forget the morning that two female hyenas decided to pick on a male lion from the pride we'd been following. He was a big lion, but he was intimidated by them. Hyenas are incredibly perceptive. They could tell he was scared simply by watching the way the lion lowered his head and tucked in his hindquarters. They chased him around, whooping and calling and nipping at him.

From afar, we could see the lion's brother sprinting in our direction. Since we were familiar with the brother—and knew that he had little patience for hyenas—we were not surprised by what happened next. He charged one of the hyenas, chasing after her at full speed. Within seconds, he had taken her down. It was a great loss for the hyena clan—she was their leader. From just a few feet away, we had captured it all on film—the ancient feud between lions and hyenas.

Giraffes at twilight

CHAPTER FOUR

ANIMAL MYSTERIES

>>> SCIENTISTS ARE THE DETECTIVES OF THE NATURAL WORLD. They spend much of their time trying to uncover the answers to mind-boggling questions about our universe. Many of these puzzles involve animals. For example, everyone knows that zebras have stripes, but did you ever wonder why? And what about a giraffe's long neck? Sure, it helps the animal reach the highest leaves, but is that its main purpose?

To figure out answers to these questions and others, scientists observe animals in the wild and conduct experiments. Sometimes, their discoveries match their predictions. Other times, what they find out is completely unexpected. And, of course, many mysteries are still waiting to be solved. We may never have all the answers, but we'll never stop digging, either!

THE GIRAFFE'S LONG NECK

How did the giraffe get such a long neck?

>>> **A GIRAFFE'S NECK IS THE LONGEST IN THE ANIMAL KINGDOM—BY A LONG SHOT!** Reaching a length of more than six feet (1.8 m), its super-stretched-out neck allows a giraffe to grab leaves at the tops of trees that other herbivores can't reach. That's why the giraffe's neck is so long, right? Maybe. The famous naturalist Charles Darwin proposed that theory more than a century ago. But not all scientists agree. Why else would an herbivore's neck evolve to be so long? Here are a few different theories.

Long Neck? Long Legs!

A giraffe's neck is extraordinarily long, but so are its front legs. It was once thought that the giraffe's neck grew so that the animal could reach down past its own legs to sip water. But that theory was dropped when archaeologists found fossils of giraffe ancestors with long legs and a short neck. Those long-legged animals drank water for millions of years—and they did it without the help of a superlong neck.

Splaying its legs is the only way for a giraffe to get a drink.

Reaching for Leaves?

Darwin's theory seems like a safe assumption, but much of the time, giraffes don't eat the highest leaves. Instead, they do most of their feeding at shoulder height, with their necks at an angle. This has led some scientists to question the idea that a giraffe's long neck is primarily for feeding.

Battle of the Giants

Some say the giraffe's long neck evolved for fighting. Male giraffes compete for females by "necking"—each swinging his neck to whack the other with his head. It could be that having a longer neck is an advantage in these battles.

Keeping Cool

Could it be that having a long neck helps a giraffe stay cool? A giraffe's tall, slender shape allows the animal to stand so that most of its body isn't exposed to the sun's hot rays. A wide animal, on the other hand, does not have this advantage. On a bright day, no matter how an elephant positions itself, a large portion of its skin is in the sun. Long legs also help giraffes beat the heat. They lift a giraffe's body high above the hottest part of its environment—the ground.

SEEING SPOTS

A giraffe's spots are like fingerprints—no two giraffes have the same pattern. These brown patches act as camouflage. They also help regulate body temperature. There are more heat-releasing blood vessels under the patches than anywhere else on a giraffe.

THE LION'S MANE

Why do male lions have manes?

>>> **IF YOU WERE ASKED TO DESCRIBE A LION, WHICH FEATURES WOULD YOU THINK OF FIRST?**

The lion's mane might be high on your list. Lions—and male lions, in particular—are the only big cats that have manes. But what is the purpose of this face-framing fluff?

A big, thick mane helps protect a lion's neck during fights with other males. It also ensures that a male lion guarding its territory can be seen from afar, a reminder to other lions to keep their distance. A lion's mane offers clues about the animal's age and health, too. Scientists had long wondered: Do lions look at other lions' manes to size each other up? In the 1990s, a team of researchers came up with a creative experiment to find out.

A male lion patrols his territory.

Make-Believe Manes

The researchers asked a toy company to make life-size stuffed lions with detachable manes of different lengths and colors. They placed the fake lions close to real lions in the Serengeti. Then they lured the real lions to the stuffed ones by playing a recording of hyenas at a kill. It worked! The lions followed the sound of the hyenas, hoping to snag a free meal. Instead of food, they found the stuffed lions.

How the real lions approached the fake ones depended on the length and color of the fake manes. A short, light-colored mane can be a sign of recent injury. Spotting an easy target, male lions were more likely to approach—and even attack—a stuffed lion with a short or light-colored mane. Female lions, on the other hand, showed interest in the fake lions that looked like better mates. They were more likely to approach one that had a darker mane—a sign of maturity and good nutrition. It seemed that the scientists' hunch was correct: Lions do look at manes. And they do so mane-ly to measure each other up.

A lioness approaches a stuffed lion.

A **LION'S MANE** can be short or long and can range in color from almost white to nearly black.

WHERE THE MALES HAVE NO MANES

In the Tsavo region of Kenya, many male lions lack manes. Why are their manes missing? Some scientists think the fluffy fur was simply snagged by thorny plants. Others have suggested the mane-less lions might belong to their own subspecies. Another possibility: Tsavo lions could simply grow their manes later in life.

MORE MANES

Check out three more mammals with manes.

When an **AARDWOLF** senses danger, it raises its mane to look bigger and more threatening.

A **WILDEBEEST** can have a shaggy or spiky mane.

A **ZEBRA'S** mane features black and white stripes.

HONEY FINDERS

How do honeyguide birds learn to lead humans to hidden beehives?

>>> LONG AGO, AFRICAN HUNTERS AND BIRDS CALLED HONEYGUIDES WORKED OUT A SWEET ARRANGEMENT. The birds would lead the people to hidden beehives. In return, the people would give the birds a treat to eat—not honey, as you'd expect, but beeswax! The exchange made perfect sense. To find honey-filled hives, the people needed the birds. To get beeswax from the hives, the birds needed the people. Working together, both humans and birds got what they wanted.

It's been hundreds of years—possibly even longer—since hunters first called on honeyguides for help. The practice has largely died out, but some people still rely on the wild birds to help them find honey. The Yao of northern Mozambique are one such group. Young Yao men summon the birds by making a *brrr hmmm* sound. The Yao say they learned the special honeyguide call from their fathers, who learned it from their fathers. But nobody knows how—or when—the *brrr hmmm* call got its start.

Even more puzzling is the question of how the birds recognize the call and know exactly what to do. The chicks aren't learning it from their parents, because their parents don't raise them. Female honeyguides lay their eggs in the nests of another bird, called a bee-eater. When the honeyguide chicks hatch, bee-eater parents take care of them. And yet, somehow, the chicks learn to do their honey-hunting job.

Male honeyguide

Honeyguide birds have been known to offer their honey-hunting assistance by flying close to people while making a **LOUD CHATTERING SOUND.**

Researchers with a male honeyguide

SHOW ME THE HONEY

Here's how the Yao work with honeyguides to uncover hidden hives.

STEP ONE: A Yao honey-hunter summons a honeyguide with the *brr hmmm* call. Then, as he follows the bird, he repeats the call, *brr hmmm*. Once the bird has located a beehive, it flicks its tail or chatters to alert its human companion.

STEP TWO: The Yao honey-hunter must get rid of the bees so they won't swarm him when he takes their hive. He prepares a bundle of wood wrapped in leaves and attaches it to a long pole. He then sets the bundle on fire and hoists it up next to the hive. The bees get a whiff of the smoke and fly away!

STEP THREE: If the nest is in a tree trunk or high up in the branches, the Yao honey-hunter cuts down the tree.

STEP FOUR: Next, he slices open the hive and scoops out the honey.

STEP FIVE: Time to reward the honeyguide. The Yao honey-hunter gathers up some wax and places it on a bed of leaves. Yum!

NARROW ESCAPE

How do some slower animals escape the speediest predators?

>>> EVEN THOUGH CHEETAHS ARE SUPERSPEEDY RUNNERS—MUCH FASTER THAN THE ANTELOPE THEY OFTEN CHASE DOWN FOR DINNER—THE QUICK CATS ONLY CATCH THEIR PREY ON ONE OUT OF EVERY THREE ATTEMPTS. How is it that slower-moving animals often manage to ditch their high-speed pursuers?

To find out, scientists looked at what happens when a cheetah chases an impala and when a lion chases a zebra. The researchers strapped movement-tracking collars onto 28 animals: five cheetahs, seven impalas, nine lions, and seven zebras. Over several years in Botswana, the collars recorded thousands of high-speed chases.

A cheetah's keen eyesight helps it judge how far it must run to reach its prey. The cat is known to **HUNT MOSTLY DURING THE DAY** because it has poor night vision.

A cheetah cub chases a Thomson's gazelle.

Surprise Exit

The recordings showed an interesting result. The impalas and zebras typically ran at only half their top speed when trying to escape predators. Moving at a slower pace allowed the animals to make a sharp turn at the last moment, just as their pursuers were closing in. Such an unexpected twist was sometimes enough to throw off a predator in the heat of a chase.

Scientists say the animals have evolved together, all growing stronger and faster over time. Both predators and prey are shaped by the challenges they encounter in their fight for survival. Lions and cheetahs must catch up with their prey so they can eat. Impalas and zebras need to make a getaway so they don't get eaten.

The lesson? The next time you find yourself in a close game of tag, you may not need to crank up the speed. Instead, slow down a bit, let your pursuer get ever so close, and then make a quick turn. It's worth a try. And even if it doesn't work, take solace in the fact that you didn't end up in a lion's mouth.

HOW **FAST?**

These days, scientists can use high-tech tracking devices to find out how quickly different animals run. But not long ago, this technology wasn't available. Researchers would sometimes drive beside running animals while watching their vehicle's speedometer. In 1997, a scientist measured a cheetah's speed by timing the cat as it covered a 656-foot (200-m) course. The cheetah was clocked running nearly 65 miles an hour (105 km/h) as it tried to catch up with a vehicle towing a piece of meat. Even without the latest gadgets, experts managed to capture a cheetah's incredible speed.

A ZEBRA'S STRIPES

Why do zebras have stripes?

Running zebras kick up dust.

>>> **FOR AN ANIMAL TRYING TO AVOID PREDATORS, HAVING AN EYE-CATCHING COAT SEEMS FAR FROM IDEAL.** So, what is the purpose of the zebra's striking pattern? The answer to this age-old question isn't black and white. In fact, stripes might help zebras in more ways than one.

Fly By, Biting Flies!

When bugs approach black or brown horses, they slow down before making a careful landing. But when flies get close to a zebra, they seem to be thrown off by the stripes. Instead of slowing down, they often fly right by or bounce off. Stopping these bugs in their tracks is beneficial, because Africa's horseflies and tsetse flies spread diseases that can be deadly to zebras.

Oh, It's You!

Much like a fingerprint, each zebra's patterned coat is unique. Zebras' stripes are believed to help the animals keep track of who's who in the herd. A young zebra also might rely on its mother's special set of stripes to pick her out from the crowd.

Seeing Stripes

Although black and white stripes stand out to us, that may not be the case for the lions and hyenas that prey on zebras. A stripy pattern might camouflage a zebra by breaking up the outline of its body. It's also possible that when zebras run in a group, stripes make the animals appear to blend together, making it a challenge for a predator to pick out a single animal.

CLIMATE CONTROL

Could a zebra's stripes help keep the animal cool? Scientists tested the theory by covering water-filled barrels with furry hides from different animals. The researchers used solid-color hides as well as patterned ones, including a hide with zebra stripes. When the barrels were left out in the sun, the zebra-striped hide did not keep the water any cooler than the other hides. Still, it's possible that a striped coat functions differently on a zebra than on a barrel—and does indeed help regulate the animal's temperature.

SOMETHING FISHY

What causes so many fish to die in East Africa's Mara River?

When food is hard to come by, hippos can **SURVIVE FOR WEEKS WITHOUT EATING.**

>>> **THE MARA RIVER FLOWS THROUGH THE SERENGETI IN EAST AFRICA, SUPPORTING MILLIONS OF ANIMALS,** including about 4,000 hippos that spend their days wallowing in the water. At night, these hippos make their way to land to feed on grass for hours. Then they return to the river.

Hippos rest on the shore of the Mara River.

Hippos by the Mara River

Stinky Cycle

Scientists studying the Mara River were stumped. Whenever the water rose by a few feet, dead fish would appear along one long stretch of the river—sometimes by the thousands. Locals suspected that pesticides trickling into the water from nearby farms were to blame, but that was just a hunch.

The scientists ran tests on the water in the areas where hippos congregate, called hippo pools. On a typical day, hippos deposit about 18,000 pounds (8,165 kg) of poop into the water. They found that where hippo waste piles up, the water is starved of oxygen and full of toxic chemicals. During heavy rains, hippo pools overflow, sending putrid water downstream. The result: River water with so little oxygen that fish cannot survive.

But the Mara River ecosystem quickly bounces back. Vultures and crocodiles eat the dead fish. The hippo poop gets flushed away by the moving water. And oxygen from the air is absorbed into the river. Within about eight hours, the river's oxygen levels return to normal. All that hippo poop may not be cause for concern—unless, of course, you're a fish.

A DANGEROUS JOURNEY

Each year, more than a million wildebeests travel some 1,800 miles (2,897 km) in a loop between Kenya and Tanzania. During their journey, the animals cross the Mara River multiple times. But wildebeests are not strong swimmers, and thousands of the animals drown. Their bodies nourish the Serengeti's wildlife. Crocodiles, vultures, and hyenas eat the carcasses. And as the bones break down, they provide nutrients for the bacteria and algae that, in turn, are a source of food for fish in the water. Scientists say it is all part of the river's natural cycle.

A herd of migrating wildebeests

CREATURE BITES

Chew on seven bite-size animal mysteries!

Some black-bellied seedcrackers have small beaks; others have large beaks. **WHY?**

Large-beaked seedcrackers eat harder seeds than their smaller-beaked counterparts. The greater the proportion of hard-shelled seeds in an area, the more large-beaked seedcrackers there are.

A cow says moo. A sheep says baa. What does a **GIRAFFE SAY?**

It was long thought that the giraffe didn't have a sound of its own. But researchers recorded giraffes overnight and discovered that the animals hum—but at a frequency too low for humans to hear.

Why do predators of puff adders often fail to **DETECT THE SNAKES?**

Like many snakes, puff adders make use of camouflage, blending in with their surroundings. But scientists found that the snakes also benefit from something known as chemical crypsis. In other words, they are completely unsmellable!

Why do some male chimpanzees
FLING HUGE ROCKS
at tree trunks?

The mysterious behavior has been recorded only in West Africa. Experts say it may be a display of strength or a way of marking territory.

Why do elephants have such
WRINKLY SKIN?

An elephant doesn't have sweat glands. To keep cool, it covers its skin in water or mud—and wrinkled skin traps moisture better than smooth skin does.

HOW do so many large, plant-eating animals have enough to eat on the African savanna?

Though elephants, zebras, impalas, and buffalo all eat plants, each species has its favorites. By analyzing each animal's poop, scientists were able to learn how the herbivores' diets differ.

Does a bichir fish really **BREATHE AIR** from the holes on its head as scientists suggested more than 100 years ago?

Yes! A recent study found that the fish inhales air through the two holes on the top of its head up to 93 percent of the time. The rest of the time, it breathes through its gills.

THAT'S BATTY!

Millions of bats meet in one tiny forest every year. Where do they all come from?

>>> **AS THE SUN SETS OVER KASANKA NATIONAL PARK IN ZAMBIA, A FEW LARGE BATS TAKE TO THE SKY.** Within moments, there are more—hundreds, then thousands, and eventually millions. The sky darkens as the bats zip around, squealing and flapping their wings. After resting all day, they are wide awake—and ready to eat.

It may sound like a scene from a scary movie, but those who have witnessed the spectacle in person say it's nothing short of magnificent. The bats themselves are far from creepy. Known as straw-colored fruit bats, they dine on flowers, leaves, and, of course, fruit. With silky fur and big orange eyes, they resemble little dogs—that is, if you're not looking at their giant wings. Unfurled, a fruit bat's wings are nearly three feet (1 m) wide. No wonder they are also known as megabats!

Straw-colored fruit bat

Fruit Loop

To see the bats gather at Kasanka, you have to pick your dates carefully. They are at the national park for only a few months each year. They begin to arrive at the end of October. A month later, there are at least eight million, all packed into a patch of forest roughly the size of two American football fields. By early January, the bats have vanished. Where exactly they go, nobody knows.

But the reason the bats come to Kasanka is no mystery. At the end of the year, the trees there are bursting with fruit. During the bats' stay at the national park, they spend their days roosting in clusters in the trees of the swampy forest. At night, they fly and feast, consuming as much as twice their own weight in fruit.

The bats aren't the only ones that benefit from their annual stay in Kasanka. As they gobble up fruit, they also swallow the seeds inside. The bats digest the seeds and scatter them in their droppings near and far, ensuring the growth of many more trees—and plenty of delicious fruit.

Straw-colored fruit bats in flight at Kasanka National Park

THE KASANKA BAT MIGRATION:
BY THE NUMBERS

Number of bats: About **8 MILLION**

Fruit eaten each night: About **6,000 TONS** (5,443 t)

Moment of
AHHH!?!!

"We filmed and photographed as this lioness blasted through water in the Okavango Delta, chasing buffalo. We've followed her for more than 10 years."

—Beverly and Dereck Joubert

LOST AT SEA

Why are great whites disappearing from South Africa's False Bay?

>>> **IT'S A SCENE THAT HAS PLAYED OUT MANY TIMES IN THE FAMOUS FALSE BAY, JUST OFF THE COAST OF CAPE TOWN, SOUTH AFRICA.** The surface of the water explodes as a shark rockets into the air, clutching a seal in its sawlike teeth. The great whites here have learned to bolt straight up to catch seals swimming near the water's surface. The predators' momentum can carry them 10 feet (3 m) into the air.

Over the years, thousands of people have traveled to the tip of South Africa and boarded boats to witness the "flying sharks" in action. But starting in 2015, great white sightings began to drop dramatically. Both scientists and shark tourism operators noted the change.

A great white shark pursues a seal in South Africa's False Bay.

Young great white sharks eat fish, including other sharks. **MATURE GREAT WHITES PREFER SEA MAMMALS,** such as sea lions and seals.

Predators Lost

What's behind the mysterious disappearance of False Bay's great whites? There are a few theories. Orcas, which have been known to feed on great whites, were spotted in the area. The great whites may have fled as a result. Another possible culprit is the fishing industry. Large fishing boats may have whisked away so many fish that hungry great whites had to leave in search of more food. They can't survive on seals alone.

When a top predator vanishes from an ecosystem, there are bound to be consequences. For example, populations of prey species can increase dramatically. But nobody could have predicted what happened at False Bay. As the sightings of great whites declined, another type of shark started turning up in its place. That shark—the sevengill—is known as a living fossil. Like its prehistoric shark ancestors, it has seven gill slits on each side, hence its name. (Most modern sharks have five gill slits.)

Will the great whites ever return to False Bay? Many people are holding out hope. In the meantime, the sevengills are making themselves right at home.

SIZING UP SHARKS

See how great whites and sevengills measure up. If great whites return to False Bay, the sevengills might have to leave the area. Otherwise, scientists say, the great whites would prey on them.

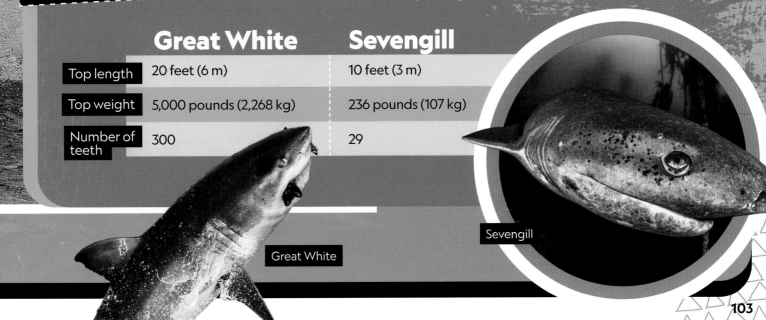

	Great White	**Sevengill**
Top length	20 feet (6 m)	10 feet (3 m)
Top weight	5,000 pounds (2,268 kg)	236 pounds (107 kg)
Number of teeth	300	29

Great White

Sevengill

JOURNEY WITH THE JOUBERTS

THROUGH A ZEBRA'S EYES

THESE DAYS, IF YOU WANT TO FILM ANIMALS ON THE SAVANNA FROM AN INTERESTING ANGLE, YOU CAN SET UP A CAMERA AT THE WATER HOLE AND STAND BACK. But when we started filming zebras in the 1980s, that technology didn't exist. We were determined to get up close and film the herd we were following without being noticed, so we came up with a makeshift disguise—a zebra-striped blanket with a hole cut out of the middle. It worked! Taking turns wearing the blanket, we were able to blend in with the zebras and capture their interactions.

One day, we witnessed an unusual rescue. The herd had migrated to an area of the Kalahari Desert where mineral-rich grass is abundant during the wet season. As we watched the zebras moving along together, we noticed something concerning. A female had died, and her little foal was on its own. The young zebra walked right up to us, searching for protection. We worried for him, but we would never intervene and disrupt the natural interactions of wild animals.

Male zebras don't typically look after the little ones, so we were surprised when we saw a stallion leave the rest of the herd to fetch the foal. At first, the young zebra wouldn't go with him. But the stallion clearly had a plan, and he wasn't giving up. He circled the small zebra, gently nudging him to get his attention. Finally, after hours of trying, the stallion won the foal's trust. The pair disappeared into the darkness to join the other zebras, and we breathed a sigh of relief.

We continued filming the herd, working around the clock to capture their lives. We stayed with them during the day. At night, we followed lions, since the big cats prey on zebras in the dark. But we realized we needed to take a different approach. By filming lions hunting zebras, we were telling a one-sided story. To truly understand the zebras' perspective, we needed to experience the dark hours through their eyes.

In the dark of night, we drove close to the herd, and Dereck got out of our vehicle. He walked through the tall grass, no more than 10 or 15 paces behind the zebras. He heard what they heard, and felt what they felt. Every time a blade of grass moved, he nearly jumped, knowing it could be a lion approaching. That night, Dereck experienced the state of high alert that is a constant for zebras, particularly in the dark hours when they could be preyed upon. It was a reminder of how eye-opening it can be to put ourselves in someone else's skin, striped as it may be.

CHAPTER FIVE

ANIMAL MYTHS BUSTED!

>>> **YOU MAY HAVE HEARD THAT AN OSTRICH TRIES TO HIDE BY BURYING ITS HEAD IN THE SAND, THAT HIPPOS ARE EXCELLENT SWIMMERS, AND THAT HYENAS ARE SCAVENGERS THAT COLLECT SCRAPS RATHER THAN HUNT FOR THEIR OWN MEALS.** These "facts" have been circulated for years. There's just one problem—they're not true!

   Where does this sort of misinformation come from? Sometimes, it's because things aren't as they seem. Though an ostrich may often appear to have its head in the sand, scientists who study the birds say they have other reasons for ducking down, such as tending to their eggs. Hippos spend most of their time in the water, but careful observation has shown that the animals don't actually swim. And studying hyenas has revealed that these carnivores are not only able to hunt, but that they do so often. Ready to uncover oodles of unexpected creature facts and features? Let's go!

A hippo aggressively displays its tusklike teeth.

MOST MISUNDERSTOOD

These creatures get a bad rap, and experts say it's undeserved.

The **LARGE, ROUNDED EARS** of African wild dogs allow the animals to detect prey from a distance and help them cool off on hot days.

Hyenas

Hyenas certainly don't win any prizes for popularity. People have long thought of the carnivores as sneaky scavengers. Even in works of fiction, from ancient tales to modern movies, hyenas are portrayed as vicious and dim-witted. But those who study them say the creatures are simply misunderstood. For one thing, hyenas aren't just scavengers. They do dine on the leftovers of other predators, but they kill most of their food.

One type of hyena, the spotted hyena, may be one of the smartest carnivores of all. These hyenas are extraordinarily social, and getting by in a complex social world takes brain power. Spotted hyenas live in clans of up to 80 individuals, with a female leader. A clan has a strict power structure, and every hyena knows its place. Low-ranking hyenas will sometimes give an alarm cry during a feeding frenzy to make others flee so there's more food to go around.

Spotted hyenas have also shown their smarts in experiments. When given a steel box with food inside, the animals use trial and error to figure out how to slide a bolt to open the door. Smart, social, and not simply scavengers—what other surprises do hyenas have in store?

Hyena pups

African Wild Dogs

The African wild dog—labeled "the Devil's dog" by some farmers—has a reputation for being a ruthless killer. Wild dogs are indeed successful hunters, taking down as many as three out of four prey they target. But many say the carnivore's bad rap is undeserved. Wild dogs are both social and generous. The animals live and hunt in packs, and always allow the puppies to feed first. If an injury prevents a member of the pack from joining the hunt, healthy individuals share their meal by regurgitating some food when they return to the den. To boost the endangered carnivore's reputation, conservationists have renamed it the "painted dog" to better describe the beauty in these spotted, tricolor predators.

Vultures

Vulture. People use the word as an insult to refer to someone who preys off the misfortunes of others. And it's no wonder why. In the wild, vultures soar through the skies, searching for dead animals to feast upon. But while eating rotting carcasses may sound gross, in doing so, vultures clean up the environment and help prevent diseases from spreading.

Many people are not aware of the important role that vultures play—or that vultures are in trouble. A recent study found that Africa's vulture population has declined drastically over the past few decades. Sometimes, the birds are poisoned by mistake. For example, people poison carcasses to kill predators, like hyenas, that attack their livestock, and vultures that feast on these carcasses are poisoned, too. Vultures have also been targeted by elephant poachers. The illegal hunters poison the elephant carcasses to kill the birds so that they will not circle overhead and catch the attention of park rangers. Conservationists are working to help vultures by spreading the word about their important role in ecosystems. They hope more people will take notice before it's too late.

Black-backed vulture

WHERE IN THE WORLD?

Some species turn up in the strangest of places.

Monkey in the Mountains

You won't find gelada monkeys swinging from leafy branch to leafy branch and eating fruits and seeds. That's because these monkeys live up high in the mountains of Ethiopia, where they spend their days plucking grass in the meadows and their nights perched on tiny cliff ledges. Sleeping on the edge of a mountain might not sound safe, but it's the monkeys' best bet for dodging prowling leopards and hyenas, which tend to hunt at night.

A male gelada sits on a cliff in Simien Mountains National Park, Ethiopia.

Sitatunga

Swamp Antelope

Frogs, turtles, and antelope: Which of these animals can be found in a swamp? If you said all three, you are correct. Though antelope are not typically swamp dwellers, the sitatunga antelope is a rare exception. With long, banana-shaped hooves, the sitatunga excels at walking on soft ground and in the water, but is a clumsy runner on dry land. The best way for sitatungas to avoid the lions and wild dogs that prey on them is to stay in the water—so stay in the water they do. They spend long hours in the deepest part of the swamp, where they sometimes sink down, leaving only their eyes and nostrils above the surface.

King of the Desert

The Namib Desert, on the southwestern coast of Africa, does not seem like an ideal place for lions. Months go by without a drop of rain. During the day, the sands can be scorching, often reaching 150°F (66°C) or more. And yet a group of about 150 lions has made their home in the punishing region. Why have they chosen to live in a place where they sometimes go weeks without water to drink? The big cats may have moved to the desert to avoid people, especially the cattle farmers who sometimes kill lions to protect their herds. It's not an easy life, but these lions have shown that they are up for the challenge.

Male lion in the Namib Desert

Penguins in Peril

Photos of penguins are often set in freezing, ice-covered Antarctica, but most types of penguins live in more temperate climates. One species can be found waddling along the southwestern coast of Africa. The African penguin is small, weighing nine pounds (4 kg) at most. A century ago, there were 1.5 million African penguins, but that number has since plummeted. Experts say the fishing industry is partly to blame, for taking too large a share of the penguins' prey. Conservationists are working to protect these special seabirds.

Penguins walk on the beach in Boulders Beach Nature Reserve, near Cape Town, South Africa.

CHOW TIME

What's on the menu? In some cases, it's not what you'd expect!

Hippopotamus

Hungry, Hungry Hippos

Hippos are huge. And just like many other giant animals, such as elephants and rhinos, they are considered vegetarians. But on occasion, some hippos have been spotted feeding on animals, including impalas, wildebeests, and zebras. Is it possible that hippos eat more meat than was previously thought? Since hippos dine at night, many of their meals go unseen by humans. It could be that some meaty items on a hippo's menu have been overlooked. On the other hand—or hoof—eating meat could simply be a last resort for hungry hippos.

The Secret Lives of Aardvarks

Studying aardvarks isn't easy. The secretive desert dwellers spend their days in burrows as deep as 32 feet (10 m) underground. When they come out at night, it is a challenge to spot them, since their eyes lack the light-reflecting surface that makes the eyes of many animals shine in the dark. Thus, an aardvark's habits are largely mysterious.

The myth that aardvarks don't ever drink and instead get all the water they need from the termites, ants, and fruit they eat circulated for years—until a group of scientists decided to dig deeper. Combing through old photographs, they found pictures of aardvarks sipping from rivers and other water sources. That put an end to the idea that aardvarks don't need to drink— one animal theory that just didn't hold water.

An aardvark investigates a termite mound for insects to eat.

A Crocodilian Diet

The Nile crocodile is known as a fierce predator, willing to take down just about anything that crosses its path. But does a croc crave a side of salad with its antelope dinner? The answer may be yes.

When researchers examined the stomach contents of 286 Nile crocodiles in Botswana's Okavango Delta, they found plants in more than one-fifth of the animals. The crocs' top greens: papyrus, grass, and seeds. Yum!

Nile crocodiles don't just eat a wide variety of foods—**THEY ALSO EAT STONES!** The stones are thought to help crocs stay buoyant in the water.

A fish makes the deadly mistake of bumping into a crocodile in the Okavango.

COLOSSAL CREATURES

These animals may be bigger than you think they are.

>>>YOU MIGHT ALREADY KNOW THAT OSTRICHES ARE THE WORLD'S LARGEST BIRDS, but did you realize that they tower over the tallest humans? Did you have any idea that a hippo could be nearly as heavy as an SUV? Find out how some surprisingly large animals measure up.

NILE PERCH VS. PIANO

400 POUNDS (181 KG)

440 POUNDS (200 KG)

AFRICAN ROCK PYTHON VS. STRETCH LIMOUSINE

30 FEET (9 M) LONG

20 FEET (6 M) LONG

GIRAFFE VS. TWO-STORY HOUSE

20 FEET (6 M) TALL

18 FEET (5.5 M) TALL

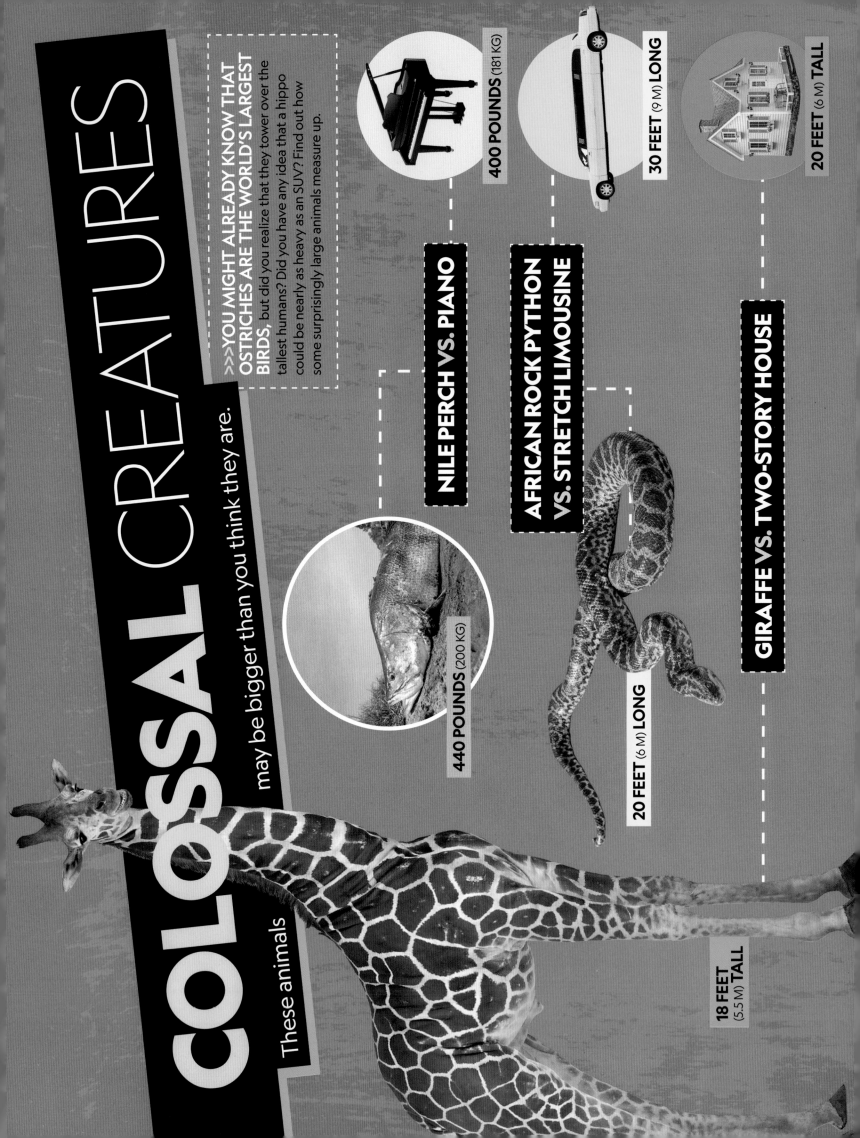

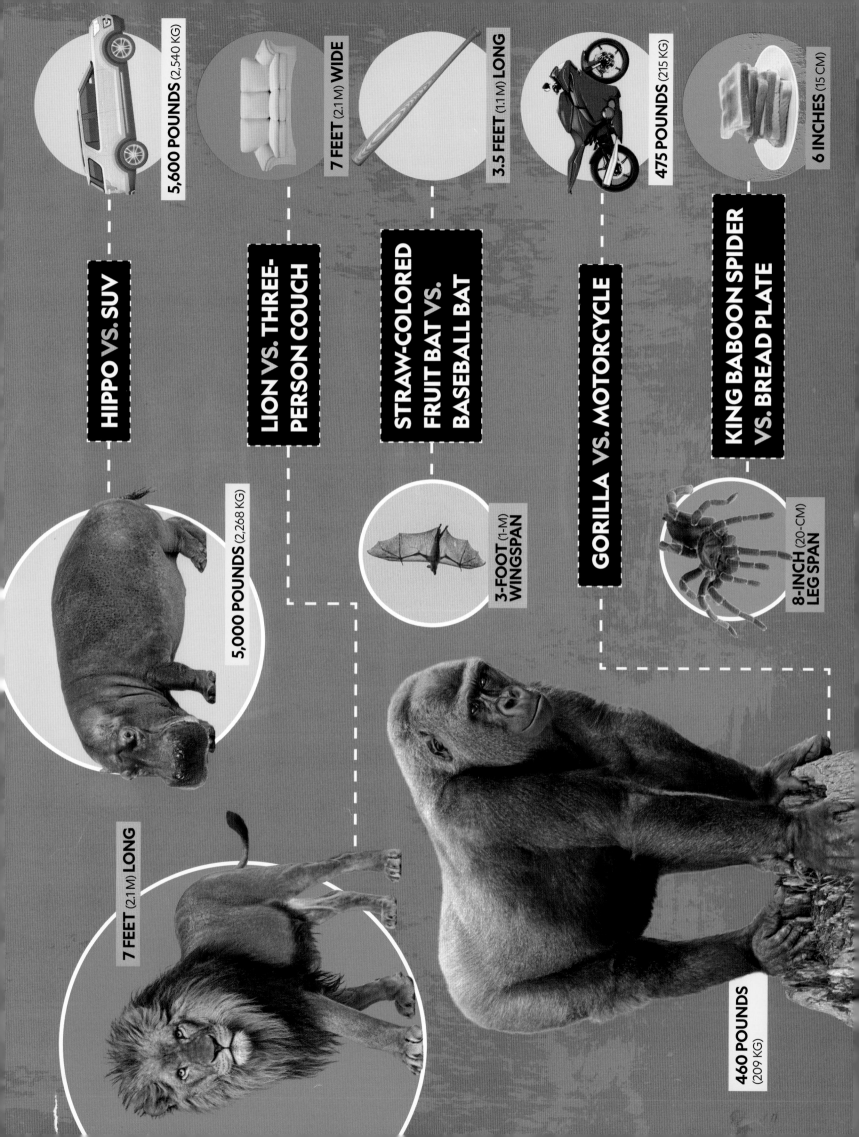

5,600 POUNDS (2,540 KG)

7 FEET (2.1 M) WIDE

3.5 FEET (1.1 M) LONG

475 POUNDS (215 KG)

6 INCHES (15 CM)

HIPPO VS. SUV

LION VS. THREE-PERSON COUCH

STRAW-COLORED FRUIT BAT VS. BASEBALL BAT

GORILLA VS. MOTORCYCLE

KING BABOON SPIDER VS. BREAD PLATE

5,000 POUNDS (2,268 KG)

3-FOOT (1-M) WINGSPAN

8-INCH (20-CM) LEG SPAN

7 FEET (2.1 M) LONG

460 POUNDS (209 KG)

CREATURE BITES

These common convictions about animals are false.

MYTH: An ostrich tries to hide by burying its head in the sand.

FACT: If an ostrich buried its head in the sand, it wouldn't be able to breathe. An ostrich may appear to have its head in the sand when it is tending to its eggs, which are in a nest in the ground.

MYTH: All reptiles hatch from eggs.

FACT: Most—but not all—reptile species lay eggs. Take the Gaboon viper, for example. This six-foot (1.8-m)-long snake mom gives birth to as many as 60 slithering babies at a time.

MYTH: Spotted hyenas laugh like people.

FACT: The high-pitch cackle, which sounds like human laughter to us, is a sound that spotted hyenas make when they are frightened or excited.

MYTH: A giraffe has an unusually large heart for an animal of its size.

FACT: A giraffe's heart is in the same proportion to its body as the heart of a dog or cow.

MYTH: A camel's hump is filled with water.

FACT: A camel's hump stores fat. When the camel is unable to find food for a long time, its body uses the stored fat for nourishment.

MYTH: Bats are blind.

FACT: Bats can see! The expression "blind as a bat" might have started because many bats search for food at night, using their ears more than their eyes. Bats find insects to eat using echolocation: They send out sound waves and wait for the echo to bounce off the objects around them.

MYTH: Meerkats eat scorpions more than any other food.

FACT: A meerkat's diet is made up mostly of tiny insects. When a meerkat is foraging, only one in 50 food items is a scorpion.

ANIMAL IQ

Some creatures show their smarts in surprising ways.

A chimpanzee eats termites off a twig.

Tools of the Trade

In 1960, primatologist Jane Goodall was observing wild chimpanzees in Tanzania when she saw something that stunned scientists all over the world. A chimp she had named David Greybeard was poking a blade of grass into a termite mound, fishing out bugs, and eating them. She knew right away that she had made a huge discovery. Until that point, scientists had thought that only humans used tools. But David the chimp, using a blade of grass as a tool to capture food, proved them wrong.

Chimps are not the only animals to use objects such as grass, sticks, and rocks as tools. Goodall later spotted Egyptian vultures in Tanzania using rocks to break open ostrich eggs. More recently, a gorilla in the Congo was filmed dipping a branch into a pool of water, as if to test how deep it was—and later using the same branch as a walking stick. Elephants are thought to use tools, too. They sometimes twitch twigs to shoo away flies and have even been seen covering up their water holes with balls of chewed-up bark, perhaps to prevent the water from drying up. Clearly, tools aren't just for primates!

Chimpanzees have **OPPOSABLE THUMBS** and **OPPOSABLE BIG TOES,** so they can grip objects with both their hands and their feet.

African gray parrot

Brainy Birds

Imagine that you have been given two closed containers and have been told that only one has nuts inside. You shake a container, and there's silence. You conclude that the other must be the one with the nuts. The task may sound simple, but most animals can't do it. Until recently, primates were the only animals thought capable of this type of reasoning. But then scientists put African gray parrots to the test. No matter which container the researchers shook first—the empty one or the one with nuts—the birds figured out which had nuts. Birdbrain: It just might be a compliment.

Magnificent Memory

You've probably heard the old saying "An elephant never forgets." It's actually true! Elephants can recognize other elephants they haven't seen in decades and can remember the locations of water sources hundreds of miles apart. But an elephant isn't the only animal with a monumental memory.

Chimpanzees can keep track of an impressive amount of information. The primates use what they know about the status of other individuals in a group to choose grooming partners. That's because grooming is about more than picking bugs off another primate's fur—it also offers a chance to form social bonds. A smart chimp makes the most of grooming time by picking a partner that will help it rise in the ranks.

Two chimpanzees groom each other.

Moment of AHHH!?!!

"We called her Tortilis, from the *Acacia tortilis* trees she loved. She was a peaceful and gentle female leopard ... mostly. On the day we took this photograph, she was very angry with her cub, who quite simply came to us for protection!"
—Beverly and Dereck Joubert

FAMILY MATTERS

These animal parents shatter expectations.

Birds of a Feather

Ostriches are the world's largest birds, so it's no surprise that their babies hatch from giant eggs that can weigh three pounds (1.4 kg) or more. What may be unexpected, though, is how ostrich parents work together to raise their young. Both parents incubate the eggs—the female during the day and the male at night. After the eggs hatch, the tag-team parenting continues, with males and females protecting chicks from predators and providing shade from the sun.

A father ostrich walks with his brood of chicks.

Snake Moms

All snakes are cold-blooded. But when it comes to parenting, at least one species is not cold-hearted. Unlike other egg-laying snakes, the southern African python mom takes care of her babies after they hatch. The python mom wraps her long body around the dozens of babies to keep them warm. But after two weeks, the mom slithers away, leaving the babies to fend for themselves.

A lioness stalks prey in tall grass.

African python

Cat's Cradle

When it comes to raising lion cubs, moms take on the lion's share of the work. Female lions also do most of the hunting for the pride. The males, however, stay busy with their own important job: defending their territory from intruders.

Babysitters Club

Male gorillas can be tough, chest-thumping animals, but at Volcanoes National Park in Rwanda, adult males often cuddle with gorilla infants. The gorillas aren't necessarily caring for their own babies, but the babysitting efforts pay off: The males that spend the most time with their group's infants end up having the most babies of their own.

A baby gorilla plays on a silverback in Volcanoes National Park in Rwanda.

Gorillas use leaves and branches to **MAKE NEW SLEEPING NESTS EACH DAY.** They go to bed when it's dark and sleep for around 12 hours a night.

CASES OF MISTAKEN IDENTITY

Some creatures are not what they were thought to be.

African wolf

Undercover Wolf

For decades, the Egyptian jackal had people scratching their heads. The issue: The supposed jackal looked suspiciously like a gray wolf. Thousands of years before, historians had noted the presence of wolves in Egypt. Scientists wondered if the ancient historians had been onto something. In 2011, they got their answer. Researchers sequenced the carnivore's DNA and discovered that it is not a jackal—it is a wolf. It's now known as the African wolf, a name that matches its true identity.

Wolves, jackals, coyotes, foxes, and dogs are all part of the same family. These animals are known as **CANIDS.**

Mermaids in Disguise?

Dugong sightings once inspired mermaid myths all over the world. Looking at a dugong, it's hard to imagine how sailors mistook the burly marine mammal for a humanlike creature, even from afar. It is easier, however, to understand how some people were tricked by dugong skeletons. The bones of the creatures' forelimbs resemble human arms. Each "arm" even has a set of five fingerlike bones.

A science magazine from 1830 tells the story of a supposed mermaid skeleton that was brought from the coast of Kenya to England. Upon inspection, it turned out to be the skeleton of a dugong. According to the writer, the body of the skeleton was quite convincing. But the skull, which looked nothing like the head of a human, was a dead dugong giveaway.

Dugong

Young male melanistic leopard, photographed with a camera trap

Blending In

"Black panther" refers to any leopard or jaguar with a dark coat. The condition that causes some wild cats to have dark fur is called melanism, and it's extremely rare among Africa's leopards. (Jaguars are not found in Africa.) Having a dark coat might help the cats blend in with their surroundings, particularly if they live in a place with many trees and plenty of shade. Black panthers are spotted so infrequently that their camouflaging coats seem to be doing the trick!

JOURNEY WITH THE JOUBERTS

THE TRUTH ABOUT
HYENAS

CURIOUS. CLEVER. PERCEPTIVE. These are the words we'd use to describe hyenas. We spent years filming them in the wild, and we realized early on that these animals were deeply misunderstood in so many ways.

When we were filming them, we'd start our workday at four in the afternoon and follow the animals throughout the night. Sometimes, we'd try to squeeze in an hour of rest in our car. It was during one of these middle-of-the-night naps that we learned the hard way just how inquisitive hyenas can be.

We awoke to a loud clunk. A hyena had climbed up into the front seat, where Beverly had left her shoes. We watched as he grabbed the shoes and started running off with them. We were living in a tent, with very few possessions, so Beverly was not prepared to let those shoes go. She leapt over her seat and jumped onto the ground to try and startle him. Fortunately, he was alone. He had such a fright that he dropped the shoes and disappeared into the night.

A Sticky Situation

That incident left us laughing. But during our months with the hyenas, Dereck once found himself in quite a bit of danger. One night, we heard hyenas making a ruckus not far from our tent. Dereck drove to the nearest water hole and found 14 of the carnivores attacking a buffalo. He got out his camera and had just started filming when a larger group of hyenas from another clan showed up. Before he knew it, there were 80 hyenas tearing into the buffalo.

Dereck wanted to capture the scene from another angle, but our lighting equipment was connected to the car battery, so he needed to reposition the vehicle. He went to move the car, but the engine wouldn't start. And soon it was evident that he didn't just have a car problem—he also had a hyena problem. As soon as Dereck realized the car wasn't turning on, the hyenas realized it, too!

They stopped what they were doing and surrounded Dereck, creeping closer and closer. Dereck had to think fast. He banged loudly on the side of the car, and that seemed to work. They started to retreat. But then they must have realized that his banging was just a bluff, because they came back.

Dereck figured he only had one more shot at scaring them off. He took a deep breath and jumped out of the car. He screamed at the top of his lungs and ran around in a frenzy. The performance convinced the hyenas—for a moment at least. All 80 bolted into the darkness. Dereck got behind the car and pushed with all his might. By some miracle, the wheels started to roll. He ran to the front of the car, jumped in, and drove away. The lesson was loud and clear: Never underestimate hyenas.

An illustration of a Deinotherium calf trying to keep up with its mother in a river

CHAPTER SIX

ANIMAL ANCESTORS

>>> **JUMP INTO YOUR TIME MACHINE.** You're about to meet the animals of Africa's past. First stop: a look at the continent's prehistoric predators. From saber-toothed cats to ferocious bear dogs, these creatures range from the beastly to the bizarre. One croc-like reptile might even have dined on dinosaurs. But don't let "SuperCroc" scare you—it's been extinct for more than 100 million years.

You'll then meet the prehistoric relatives of today's enormous herbivores. Did you know that there used to be many more giant mammals roaming the African continent? Some were even bigger than their modern counterparts.

Though most of these creatures were gone long before humans walked the planet, we know about them thanks to the fossilized teeth and bones they left behind. Paleontologists study these prehistoric clues to figure out how ancient animals lived and what they looked like. Fossils also show us how creatures have evolved to become the amazing animals we know today.

PREHISTORIC PREDATORS

Some predators from the past were so strange that they could easily be mistaken for imaginary creatures. Here's a look at five bizarre beasts whose fossils have been found in Africa.

The **FIRST RUBIDGEA FOSSIL** was found in the 1930s on a farm in what is now South Africa.

Illustration of *Rubidgea* with prey in what is now South Africa

NAME: **Rubidgea**

WHEN IT LIVED: 256–255 million years ago

WHAT WE KNOW: Is it a dinosaur? Is it a cat? No, it's *Rubidgea,* a fearsome predator with teeth longer than those of the famous *Tyrannosaurus rex! Rubidgea* was part of a group of reptiles called therapsids, which started developing mammal-like features long before the appearance of actual mammals. One example: long limbs that made it easier for the animals to move over rough terrain.

NAME: Cynognathus

WHEN IT LIVED: 248–240 million years ago

WHAT WE KNOW: In South Africa 245 million years ago, this creature was the closest thing to today's dog. The seven-foot (2.1-m)-long predator was part of a group of mammal-like reptiles called cynodonts. In these creatures, a plate of bone across the top of the mouth separated food passages from breathing passages so they could eat and breathe at the same time—just as we can.

NAME: Hyainailouros sulzeri

WHEN IT LIVED: 22–18 million years ago

WHAT WE KNOW: Heads up! This giant meat-eater had a skull twice the size of a lion's and a mouth full of bone-crushing teeth. Since its paws were not built for grabbing prey, the creature is thought to have been more of a scavenger than a hunter.

NAME: Amphicyon giganteus

WHEN IT LIVED: About 17 million years ago

WHAT WE KNOW: The carnivore known as the bear-dog was neither a bear nor a dog, but it resembled both animals. *Amphicyon giganteus* was about the same size as a brown bear is today. The agile predator had sharp teeth and powerful jaws specially adapted for slicing meat and cracking bones.

NAME: Homotherium latidens

WHEN IT LIVED: 5–0.5 million years ago

WHAT WE KNOW: This powerful cat must have had a distinctive trot, since its front limbs were quite a bit longer than its hind limbs. It had bladelike canines, known as saber teeth, for biting into the throat of its prey. Like the lion, this cat is thought to have hunted in groups to bring down large animals.

MEET SUPERCROC

This monstrous reptile was built for the hunt.

>>> AROUND 110 MILLION YEARS AGO, THE SAHARA LOOKED VERY DIFFERENT FROM HOW IT APPEARS TODAY. Instead of bone-dry sand dunes, there was a lush jungle with winding rivers. Dinosaurs ruled the land. And the water was home to a particularly monstrous reptile—a crocodile ancestor large enough and powerful enough to feast on dinosaurs. The bus-length beast has been dubbed Super-Croc, but its official name is *Sarcosuchus* (SARK-oh-SOOK-us), which means "flesh crocodile." Like its modern relatives, SuperCroc was an ambush predator, skilled at surprising its prey and chomping down with bone-crushing force. From snout to tail, here's what made SuperCroc the perfect predator.

Colossal Croc

Tipping the scales at more than eight tons (7 t), the croc was 10 times heavier than any of its modern relatives—and at up to 40 feet (12 m), it was also twice as long. Experts say the reptile took about 40 years to reach its full size and that it might have had a life span of 100 years!

Built-In Armor

The croc was protected from head to mid-tail in a sheath of bony plates covered in skin. These plates are called scutes. Like the cross section of a tree trunk, each scute features annual growth rings that reveal the animal's age.

Eyes On Top

The croc's eyes sat high on its head and tilted upward, allowing the reptile to keep its body submerged in the river as it scanned its surroundings for possible prey.

Super Sensors

Special receptors lining the jaw could sense the tiniest movement, helping the croc pick up on the presence of prey large and small—and then pounce!

Strange Snout

A bony growth called a bulla protruded from the tip of the croc's snout. What was its purpose? Nobody knows. Scientists speculate that the bulla might have been used to determine the location of a scent—helpful because a stiff-necked croc can't turn its head. Another theory is that the bulla enhanced the reptile's calls, helping it communicate with crocs near and far.

Terrible Teeth

The croc's jaws were lined with more than 100 razor-sharp teeth. With them, the reptile was able to tear into whatever type of prey it craved. Experts say the croc's menu probably included just about anything unlucky enough to cross its path, from five-foot (1.5-m)-long prehistoric fish to young dinosaurs drinking water at the river's edge.

Jaws of Steel

Crocodiles are known for their ability to bite down hard. Scientists say *Sarcosuchus*'s bite was so powerful that forcing open its jaws would be equivalent to lifting 18,000 pounds (8,165 kg). Once the reptile's jaws clamped shut, it was impossible for prey to escape.

MEGA-BEASTS

These prehistoric plant-eaters were huge!

》》 A MEGA-HERBIVORE IS EXACTLY WHAT YOU'D GUESS—AN ENORMOUS PLANT-EATING MAMMAL. More specifically, it's one that weighs more than 2,000 pounds (907 kg). Today, Africa is home to five mega-herbivores: elephants, hippos, giraffes, and white and black rhinos. But the continent used to have many more. Why did most of these giants go extinct? Scientists aren't sure.

It was long assumed that human ancestors were to blame for overhunting the animals. But a newer theory says climate change was the culprit. As the climate began to shift around four million years ago, many of Africa's forests were replaced by grasslands. Over time, certain animals that ate leaves but not grass disappeared along with their food sources.

The complete story of these creatures might remain cloaked in mystery. But by studying the fossils the animals left behind, paleontologists can piece together how they might have looked—and lived. Here's a look at four mega-beasts that once ruled the land.

Jumbo Giraffe

The giraffe family used to be much bigger. Today, there are two species—giraffes and okapis—but paleontologists have uncovered the bones of dozens more. The fossils of a particularly burly giraffe ancestor called *Sivatherium* have been found in Africa, Europe, and Asia. At first, experts studying the creature's huge skull and cumbersome horns thought the animal might have been as heavy as an elephant. Now scientists have a different take. A recent study put the animal's weight at a maximum of 4,000 pounds (1,814 kg)—still hefty, but not nearly as massive as an elephant. Ancient rock paintings in the Sahara are thought to depict the prehistoric creature. These have led some experts to conclude that *Sivatherium* was hunted to extinction.

Sivatherium

Turned-Around Tusks

Elephants are massive, but compared to some of their prehistoric relatives, today's elephants are lightweights. *Deinotherium* was one such trunk-toting herbivore. Though individuals found in Africa were about the same size as modern elephants, fossils unearthed in Europe and Asia reveal ancient animals that were three times as heavy. *Deinotherium* was distinct from elephants in that it had no upper tusks. Instead, its tusks protruded from its lower jaw and curved inward toward the animal's body. Scientists aren't sure how the animal used its unusual tusks!

Deinotherium

Pelorovis

Eye Spy

Thanks to the placement of its eyes, a hippo can see even when it is mostly underwater. But one hippo ancestor took head-topping eyes to another level—literally! *Hippopotamus gorgops* had eyes jutting from the top of its skull, like little antennae. Though the ancient hippo may have been longer and heavier than its modern-day relatives, it was virtually invisible when it lurked like a submarine underwater.

Longhorn

Pelorovis had been extinct for hundreds of thousands of years when a paleontologist gave the animal its name, which means "monstrous sheep." At up to 4,400 pounds (2,000 kg), this animal certainly would have been monstrous, but a careful study of its bones later revealed that *Pelorovis* was not a member of the sheep family after all. Instead, it was an ancient relative of the African buffalo, although taller and heavier than a modern buffalo. But the difference that sticks out the most is the extinct creature's enormous set of curving horns. In the largest individuals, these horns may have spanned more than 10 feet (3 m) across—too wide to fit through a garage door!

Hippopotamus gorgops

Not a Horse, of Course

The burly herbivore *Ancylotherium,* with a horse's face, a rhinolike body, and claws rather than hooves, might just be the ultimate mammal mash-up. Adding to its bizarre appearance were its extra-long front limbs. Scientists think *Ancylotherium* used them to pull down tree branches to eat the leaves. This animal lived in eastern Africa as recently as two million years ago, but no living members of its family remain today.

Ancylotherium

PAST vs. PRESENT

Compared to their prehistoric relatives, some animals are pip-squeaks! See how five modern creatures stack up against their ancient counterparts.

BONE-CRACKING CARNIVORES

PACHYCROCUTA/GIANT HYENA
39 INCHES (100 CM) TALL (AT SHOULDER)
250 POUNDS (113 KG)

ENORMOUS ELEPHANTS

DEINOTHERIUM
14 FEET (4 M) TALL
19 TONS (17 T)

AFRICAN ELEPHANT
12 FEET (4 M) TALL
7 TONS (6 T)

WARTHOG
31 INCHES (80 CM) TALL
330 POUNDS (150 KG)

SPOTTED HYENA
33 INCHES (84 CM) TALL
176 POUNDS (80 KG)

NOTOCHOERUS
47 INCHES (120 CM) TALL
992 POUNDS (450 KG)

WALLOPING WARTHOGS

SARCOSUCHUS
40 FEET (12 M) LONG
17,637 POUNDS (8,000 KG)

NILE CROCODILE
20 FEET (6 M) LONG
2,300 POUNDS (1,043 KG)

COLOSSAL CROCS

OSTRICH
9 FEET (2.7 M) TALL
330 POUNDS (150 KG)

ELEPHANT BIRD
10 FEET (3 M) TALL
1,700 POUNDS (770 KG)

BULKY BIRDS

CREATURE BITES

The fossil of a five-foot (1.5-m)-long lizard was uncovered in Egypt. It's believed to be an **ANCIENT RELATIVE** of the Komodo dragon, a reptile found only in Indonesia.

Lungfish first appeared about 400 million years ago, **LONG BEFORE THE DINOSAURS.**

There are **NO BEARS** in Africa today, but there were a few million years ago. Agriotherium looked much like a modern bear, but with **LONGER LIMBS.**

African wildcats, which were viewed as **SACRED** and commonly mummified in ancient Egypt, are believed to be the ancestors of all **HOUSE CATS.**

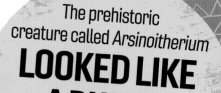

GIANT FISH called coelacanths (SEEL-uh-kanths) were thought to have **GONE EXTINCT** 65 million years ago, until one was discovered in 1938 on a fishing boat in South Africa.

The prehistoric creature called Arsinoitherium **LOOKED LIKE A RHINO,** but its horns were made of **BONE** instead of keratin.

The fossil of a **BEACH-BALL-SIZE FROG** from 70 million years ago was found on the island of Madagascar. Scientists named the creature Beelzebufo, or **"DEVIL FROG."**

Ekorus ekakeran, a **PREHISTORIC RELATIVE** of the honey badger, was as **LARGE** as a leopard.

CREATURES FROM THE NOT TOO DISTANT PAST

Experts say humans had a role in wiping out these species.

A regal, large male lion, reminiscent of the Barbary lion

>>> THE BARBARY LION, THE DODO BIRD, AND THE ELEPHANT BIRD ONCE LIVED AMONG PEOPLE. Their stories have become cautionary tales—reminders of what can happen when humans don't take steps to protect the species that need us most.

The Curious Case of the Barbary Lion

In ancient Rome, as many as 50,000 people at a time used to cram into the Colosseum to watch battles unfold before their eyes. Sometimes, lions were brought in to fight humans. These weren't just any lions either—they were a subspecies from northern Africa known as Barbary lions. The cats were admired for their size and dark manes. Over time, the Romans removed thousands of the animals from the wild, but they weren't the only ones who sought out the magnificent cats.

Barbary lions were kept as symbols of power by royal families in African countries. They were displayed in zoos and circuses in Europe. And in the 19th century, they were targeted by hunters. By the 1920s, almost all the wild Barbary lions were gone. Not one has been spotted in the wild since the 1950s. But that may not be the end of the Barbary lion's story.

Several zoos claim to have these lions. Efforts are underway to preserve the animals by breeding them. If they are indeed descendants of Barbary lions, there could still be a future for the cats.

Not a Dodo

For thousands of years, the only inhabitants of the island of Mauritius were animals. One of those creatures was a flightless bird with a big head, small wings, and short yellow legs. In the 16th century, Europeans arrived and immediately took note of the odd-looking bird. They gave it many different names. The one that stuck was "dodo," based on a Portuguese word that means "fool." But being harshly judged by humans was the least of the dodo's problems.

The settlers brought with them a variety of animals—including pigs, monkeys, and rats—that were new to the island. Scientists believe these animals ate dodo eggs and chicks and competed with the birds for other food. The settlers hunted some of the birds as well. By the end of the 17th century, every last dodo was gone. Since the bird had been driven to extinction so soon after it was discovered, some people wondered if it had existed at all. There were no cameras when the dodo was alive, so the only images of the bird are sketches and paintings that may not be completely accurate.

In recent years, scientists have studied the world's one complete dodo skeleton to uncover the truth about the bird. They say it was slimmer than it appears in drawings and faster on its feet than was previously thought. They also point out that the bird's reputation for being a "dodo" isn't deserved. After all, the bird knew just how to survive in its environment. More than 300 years since the dodo went extinct, the bird remains a reminder of the power that humans have to impact nature.

An artist's representation of dodo birds

Eyewitnesses reported that the dodo weighed as much as **50 POUNDS** (23 kg). But scientists who have studied dodo bones believe the bird was less than half that weight.

History's Biggest Bird

These days, the ostrich is the largest bird in the world. But compared to its extinct cousin the elephant bird, an ostrich is practically puny! Elephant birds lived on the island of Madagascar and were last seen in the 17th century. The flightless bird stood up to 10 feet (3 m) tall and weighed as much as 1,700 pounds (771 kg)—more than a cow. Elephant-bird eggs were enormous. They were the biggest eggs ever laid by any known animal, including dinosaurs.

When people arrived on Madagascar, they started taking the massive eggs. It's easy to understand why: At more than 150 times the volume of a chicken egg, an elephant-bird egg would have provided plenty of food. The egg-shells were also used to carry water. Experts say the stealing of these eggs might have led to the birds' extinction.

BRING THEM BACK?

It sounds like the plot of a science-fiction movie, but scientists are working on bringing extinct species back to life. The process, called de-extinction, involves inserting genes from an extinct animal into the DNA of a close living relative. For example, to bring back the extinct woolly mammoth, researchers might alter the DNA of an Asian elephant. This method would only work for animals that went extinct within the last 500,000 years, so dinosaurs are out of the question. But the dodo bird has been suggested as a candidate for de-extinction.

Some see restoring extinct animals as a way to reverse the effects of our own mistakes. They say it's our responsibility to bring back the creatures we drove off the planet. But others argue that money and energy would be better spent helping living animals that need our protection. What do you think?

An elephant bird egg reconstructed from broken fragments

JOURNEY WITH THE JOUBERTS

CREEPING CROCODILES

WHEN YOU LOOK AT CROCODILES IN THE WATER, YOU GET A SENSE THAT IF YOU WERE UNLUCKY ENOUGH TO FIND YOURSELF ENTANGLED WITH ONE, THERE WOULD BE NO MERCY. You could splash. You could yell. But the crocodile would not let go.

We've had some pretty hairy moments in the water with these reptiles. Early in our career, we were filming crocodiles in Botswana's Chobe River. After a day with the animals, we were headed back to camp in an old boat we'd borrowed from Dereck's brothers. As we turned a corner, we collided with some broken trees that had fallen into the water. One of the branches went straight through the rusty hull of the old boat, and it started to fill with water.

We had to think quickly. All our camera gear was on that boat. If we lost it, that would have been an expensive accident. Beverly quickly loaded the equipment onto an old rubber raft, and then jumped into the river and pulled the raft to the nearest island. Meanwhile, Dereck tried to salvage the damaged boat. By stuffing the hole with canvas and plastic, he managed to stop the boat from sinking. Luckily, the boat and our gear were saved—and the crocodiles kept their distance!

A Chilling Realization

That incident gave us a scare. But the time that we were most vulnerable to a run-in with crocodiles, we weren't even aware of them. We'd spent the first 10 years of our career filming in a part of Botswana where much of the water had dried up. So, when we started working along the Linyanti River, crocodiles weren't on our radar. We'd set up our tent near the water, and we'd go down to fill our tea kettle several times a day, never worrying about what could be creeping nearby.

But then, a crocodile expert visited our camp. He watched with concern as we went to collect water. That night, he took us out on his boat. With the spotlight shining, he showed us that the river was full of crocodiles. Some were 18 feet (5.5 m) long! He explained that crocodiles observe our patterns. "They are always watching," he said. "If you go down to the river six times a day, they know it. They will move in an inch at a time." With that, we installed a pump!

CHAPTER **SEVEN**

SUPER CREATURES

>>> **A RAT THAT SOAKS ITS HAIRS IN POISON. A MONKEY WHOSE FACE IS RED, GOLD, AND BLUE. A BIRD THAT SQUIRTS POOP AT ITS ENEMIES. AND A LIZARD COVERED IN POINTY SPIKES.** These are just a few of Africa's most extreme animals.

We've compiled a list of creatures that truly stand out. Some animals are included here due to their unusual abilities. Others make the cut based on their unique features. And a few are remarkable because of how they interact with other creatures. Taken together, this list offers a glimpse of the many weird, wacky, and wonderful ways animals have evolved to survive in their environments.

Being huge, spine-covered, or extra smelly can protect a creature from predators. Knowing how to work together can mean more food for everyone. And being extra colorful helps some animals find mates. How else do exceptional creatures win the race for survival? Read on to find out!

Lilac-breasted roller

SAVANNA ELEPHANT

Whoa, baby! Savanna elephants are big from Day One. A newborn calf can be a whopping 265 pounds (120 kg). By the time it's full-grown, it can weigh more than 13,200 pounds (5,987 kg), or roughly the same as a mini school bus. Maintaining the title of heaviest land animal is a full-time job. Savanna elephants spend 16 hours a day feeding, and they consume as much as 5 percent of their body weight every 24 hours. It's hard work, but they are up to the task!

MOST MASSIVE

🌐 **WHERE IT'S FOUND:** Sub-Saharan Africa

🐾 **THAT'S WILD!** The world's other two elephant species—the forest elephant and the Asian elephant—weigh thousands of pounds less than the savanna elephant.

RUNNERS-UP

HIPPO AND WHITE RHINO

These bulky beasts have both been known to tip the scales at more than 5,000 pounds (2,268 kg), though hippos tend to be heavier than rhinos. White rhinos are built for grazing and can be found throughout the day and night with their muzzles to the ground, munching away. Hippos feast on grass, too, but for them, mealtime is at night when it's cooler.

MANDRILL

Is that monkey wearing face paint? It may be hard to believe, but a male mandrill really is that colorful. Its long red nose is framed with blue skin, and its face is adorned with a golden beard. The male monkey even has red and blue skin on its rear! Hormones fuel the colors, and the highest-ranking males have the brightest hues of all. The splashy colors help these monkeys stand out to the females in their group.

MOST COLORFUL

 WHERE IT'S FOUND: Africa's equatorial rainforests

THAT'S WILD! A mandrill's cheeks have built-in pouches used for storing food.

RUNNER-UP LILAC-BREASTED ROLLER

Thanks to its feathers of many colors, a lilac-breasted roller can be spotted from a distance. The pigeon-size bird is pretty, but the sound it makes is not! Repeating "rak, rak," the roller is known for making a racket.

FUNKIEST FEATURE

WINNER!

AYE-AYE

It's rude to point, but this little primate can't help it! Each of its hands has one finger that is longer and bonier than the other four fingers. The unusual appendage looks creepy, but it has an important purpose. The aye-aye searches for insects by tapping this finger against a tree and listening for the hollow spots where bugs live. Then, after tearing away the bark with its teeth, the aye-aye uses the same extra-long finger to grab its creepy-crawly dinner.

CRESTED RAT

RUNNER-UP

When a crested rat is under attack, it doesn't run and it doesn't hide. Instead, its fur parts to reveal a special tract of straw-colored hairs that run from its ribs to its hip and are packed with deadly poison. One little taste is all it takes to fend off a predator. Since the rat can't make its own poison, it chews on the bark of a poisonous tree and then slobbers its drool onto its own spongy hairs. That's one clever way to keep predators at bay!

WHERE IT'S FOUND: Forests of Madagascar

THAT'S WILD! The aye-aye's bushy tail, which helps it balance as it scampers along tree branches, is longer than its body.

MOST SOCIAL

🏆
WINNER!

MEERKAT

There's no *I* in meerkat, and the squirrel-size mammals seem to know it. Meerkats live in groups of up to 40 and do everything together. Each morning, the animals emerge from their underground burrows and get right to work. A few babysit the newborn pups, while the rest set out in search of food. While the group sniffs around for crunchy scorpions and tasty mice, one meerkat keeps watch for predators, ready to warn the others at the first sign of danger. Working together helps the mammals survive in a harsh environment. Go, Team Meerkat!

RUNNER-UP

AFRICAN WILD DOG

Domestic dogs are known for being loyal, and their distant cousins, African wild dogs, share this quality. The carnivores do everything as a pack, from hunting to raising pups. One study found that the animals make a group decision about when to hunt—by sneezing to cast a "yes" vote. That sort of cooperation is nothing to sneeze at!

WHERE IT'S FOUND: Deserts and grasslands of southern Africa

THAT'S WILD! Meerkats are members of the mongoose family. Like other mongooses, meerkats have a natural immunity against snake and scorpion venom.

SPINIEST

WINNER!

CRESTED PORCUPINE

Even lions know better than to mess with this quilled creature. When a crested porcupine is threatened, it raises the long, spiny hairs on its head and shoulders to appear extra-large and shakes its rattle-like tail quills as if to say, "Stay away!" If that doesn't do the trick, the porcupine runs backward and drives its needle-sharp quills into its attacker. Ouch!

RUNNER-UP ## ARMADILLO LIZARD

Hands off! This rock-dwelling lizard is covered in sharp spikes from neck to tail. When threatened, it rolls itself up by gripping its tail in its mouth. The lizard remains a spine-covered ball—with its soft belly protected—until its attacker takes off.

Moment of AWWW!!!

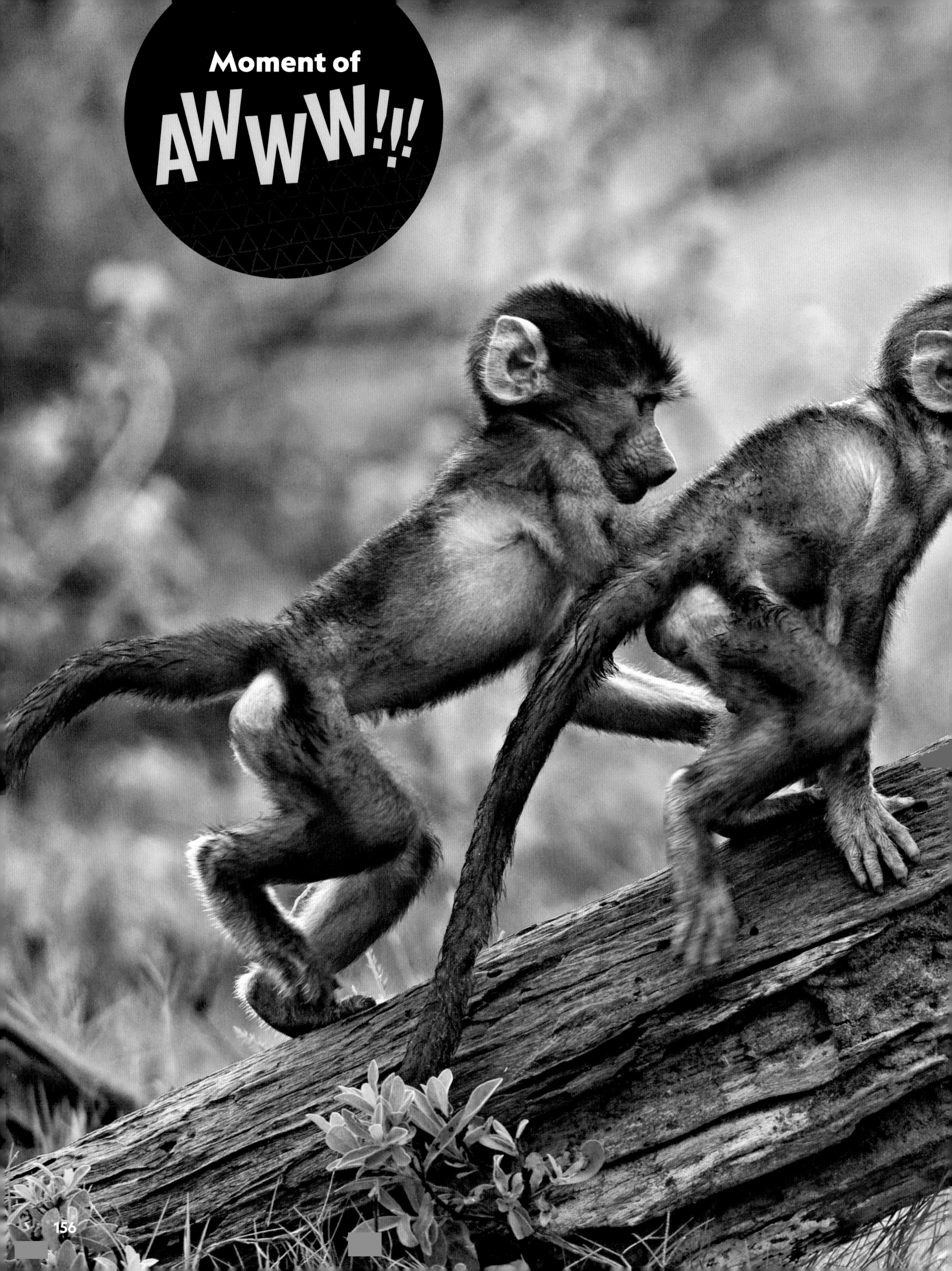

"We're never too busy to stop and film baby baboons. They're always up to something—a tail pull, rough and tumble, some kind of mischief."

—Beverly and Dereck Joubert

GUTSIEST

🏆
WINNER!

HONEY BADGER

Who's afraid of a big, bad snake? Not the honey badger! The pint-size predator is famous for feasting on Africa's deadliest serpents. It's also known to attack beehives and stand up to creatures many times its own size, including lions. With thick skin, razor-sharp teeth and claws, and a scent gland similar to a skunk's, the honey badger is well-equipped to go to battle.

RUNNER-UP

AFRICAN BUFFALO

A male buffalo's massive horns fuse together to form a forehead shield called a boss. It's an appropriate name for the headgear of a creature large and powerful enough to do pretty much whatever it pleases. African buffalo are known for being short-tempered and unpre-dictable. The massive mammals are not afraid of a fight, and also team up to defend members of the herd.

 WHERE IT'S FOUND: Sub-Saharan Africa and southern Asia

 THAT'S WILD! The honey badger is a clever creature. For its size, it has one of the largest brains of any carnivore.

SMELLIEST

GREEN WOOD HOOPOE

WINNER!

It's not easy being a green wood hoopoe. The bird is a favorite meal of the rats, snakes, and cats that share its forest habitat. But the hoopoe does have a secret weapon. When threatened, it can turn its tail toward its attacker and spray a foul-smelling oil. The solution contains the same chemical that gives rotten eggs their distinctive smell. Young green wood hoopoes can also resort to method "number two": squirting large quantities of liquid poop.

SPOTTED HYENA

RUNNER-UP

One way that spotted hyenas communicate stinks! That's because the animals send messages to each other by smearing a smelly paste onto stalks of grass. The paste reveals all sorts of information about the animal, including what clan it belongs to and whether it is male or female. And the smelly substance has staying power—even humans can detect the odor for more than a month after the paste is deposited on the grass.

WHERE IT'S FOUND: Sub-Saharan Africa

THAT'S WILD! Green wood hoopoe chicks are raised by their parents with the assistance of up to 10 helper birds.

CREATURE BITES

One **SUPERSTRONG** species of dung beetle can pull 1,141 times its own body weight—the equivalent of a 10-year-old kid being able to lift **SIX LARGE ELEPHANTS.**

Able to live up to 30 years, a naked mole rat has the **LONGEST LIFE SPAN** of any rodent.

The lion is the **LOUDEST CAT,** able to produce a thunderous **110-DECIBEL ROAR** that can be heard from five miles (8 km) away.

An elephant is pregnant for up to 22 months, the **LONGEST GESTATION** period for a mammal.

A wild giraffe sleeps about five minutes at a time, up to six times a day. That's only about **HALF AN HOUR OF SHUT-EYE** in total!

The mosquito is the world's
DEADLIEST ANIMAL.
By spreading several diseases, including malaria, which can be fatal if left untreated, the insect causes hundreds of thousands of deaths in Africa each year.

With a 60 percent hunting success rate, the tiny black-footed cat is considered the
DEADLIEST
of the entire cat family.

A pygmy mouse lemur, the world's
SMALLEST PRIMATE,
can weigh as little as 1.5 ounces (42.5 g)—roughly the same as a
GOLF BALL.

Able to reach speeds of
34 MILES AN HOUR
(55 km/h), the patas monkey is the **FASTEST**
of all the primates.

At a length of barely more than an inch (2.5 cm), Madagascar's *Brookesia micra* is the **TINIEST CHAMELEON** in the world.

SHOEBILL

With a massive beak; large, bright eyes; and a tuft of feathers sticking up from its head, the shoebill looks like a cartoon villain. But make no mistake—the shoebill is real. Just ask the lungfish—a shoebill's favorite meal. The bird stands in shallow water and waits in silence until a fish approaches. Then it uses its big beak to clamp down on its slippery prey. Turtles, lizards, and the occasional baby crocodile are also on the shoebill's menu.

PATAS MONKEY

RUNNER-UP

This mustached monkey looks like a character from a Dr. Seuss book, and in fact, it's thought to have been the inspiration for one of the author's most famous characters, the Lorax. In Seuss's story, the Lorax tries to save the forest's trees from being cut down. In real life, too, the patas monkeys' acacia trees are being cleared away, and the monkeys are disappearing—a habitat loss now as much fact as fiction.

WACKIEST-LOOKING

WHERE IT'S FOUND: Swamps of eastern Africa

THAT'S WILD! The shoebill will often begin a meal by biting off the head of its prey.

MOST MYSTERIOUS

WHERE IT'S FOUND: Sub-Saharan Africa and southern Asia

 THAT'S WILD! A pangolin has no teeth. Sand and small stones in its stomach help grind up its food.

PANGOLIN

WINNER!

Scientists are racing to learn about the secret lives of pangolins. The odd-looking insect-eaters are some of the most hunted animals in the world, sought after for their meat and scales (see pages 174–175). They are also among the most mysterious. Since pangolins are shy and nocturnal, it's a challenge to observe them in the wild. When a pangolin is threatened, it curls up in a roly-poly ball—a useful defense strategy against leopards and lions, but not against human hunters. Hopefully, researchers will unwrap the animal's secrets before it's too late.

ZENKERELLA

RUNNER-UP

No scientist has documented seeing a living Zenkerella, but the elusive rodent has been found dead in hunters' snares in the rainforests of central and West Africa. It looks like a common squirrel, but with scales at the base of its bushy tail. The scales are thought to help the animal get a better grip as it climbs trees. But until the Zenkerella can be observed in action, its way of life will remain a mystery.

MOST ACROBATIC

WINNER!

SIFAKA

Leaping lemurs! In the forests of Madagascar, sifakas bounce through the trees with such speed and precision that they appear to be flying. Unlike most other primates, these lemurs don't travel along branches. Instead, they jump from trunk to trunk in an upright position, using their hands and feet to land and then spring off again. Able to leap more than 30 feet (9 m) at a time, the sifaka is the long-jump champion of the forest.

CARACAL

RUNNER-UP

This ninja cat is a master of stealth. Once it spots its prey, it sneaks up in silence ... and then pounces! If the cat is after a bird, it can use its powerful hind legs to spring itself six feet (1.8 m) off the ground. Up in the air, it swats at its flying prey. When the injured bird comes down, it's time to dine.

 WHERE IT'S FOUND: Western and southwestern Madagascar

THAT'S WILD! The name sifaka is based on the *shif-auk* call the animal makes as it travels through the forest.

JOURNEY WITH THE JOUBERTS

ELEPHANT EMERGENCY

WHEN IT COMES TO FILMING WILDLIFE, WE TYPICALLY OPERATE LIKE FLIES ON THE WALL, WATCHING STORIES UNFOLD FROM THE SIDELINES. But there is an exception to that rule. If a human-made situation puts animals in danger, we will do what we can to turn things around.

During the dry season in Botswana in 1992, we were filming a herd of elephants that had emerged from the forest to drink from some water holes by the road. Some of these were wells that had been dug by people and were quite deep. We watched with concern as an elephant dipped its trunk down one particularly treacherous well. We were right to be worried. The situation was about to take a turn for the worse.

From the distance, we heard a vehicle approaching. As the truck came closer, we saw that a large group of passengers were riding in the back. They must have been frightened of the elephants. They started banging the sides of the truck and yelling loudly, as if to scare the animals away. Unfortunately, it worked. The animals were so startled that they ran off in a frenzy.

When the truck was gone and the herd had disappeared into the forest, we saw that there was a problem. Amid all the commotion, a calf had fallen into the deepest well, and he was stuck. Just as we were contemplating what to do, we saw that a large female—the calf's mother—was coming back. She rushed to the edge of the well but had no way of pulling the little one out. Then something remarkable happened. She walked right up to our vehicle and placed her head on the hood. Was she asking for our help? We couldn't be certain of that. But we did know she needed it. We were also aware that her problem had been caused by people. We made the decision to step in.

We drove our vehicle to the well. Dereck grabbed a long winch cable and some blankets and climbed down. He placed the blankets around the elephant to protect its skin and then wrapped the cable around the animal's body. Once the cable was securely in place, we gave it a little tug. The calf squealed in discomfort, and his mother came rushing over. It was clear that this wasn't going to be a quick and easy rescue.

Little by little, we managed to dislodge the calf. By the time we got him out of the well, it was dark, and his mother had wandered into the distance. We needed her to come back and fetch her baby. Dereck gently twisted the little elephant's tail, and he squealed once again. His mother quickly returned. She wrapped her trunk around his body, comforting him. And then they disappeared into the darkness.

African elephant

CHAPTER EIGHT

SAVING SPECIES

>>> IN CHAPTER 6, WE MET THE DODO, A UNIQUE-LOOKING BIRD THAT DIED OUT CENTURIES AGO DUE TO HUMAN ACTIONS. THE DODO IS LONG GONE, BUT THE LESSONS LEARNED FROM ITS STORY LIVE ON. When the dodo was driven to extinction, people did not realize what was happening to the species until it was too late. Today, we know much more.

We know that cutting down trees destroys habitats and harms animals. We know that releasing species into areas where they do not belong disturbs the balance within ecosystems. And we know that overhunting can wipe a species off the planet.

Fortunately, we also have the power to fix our mistakes. Through dedication, hard work, and ingenuity, conservationists are saving species in Africa and around the world. Want to know more about the challenges facing Africa's wildlife and what you can do to help? Let's get ready to rescue!

STOPPING POACHERS IN THEIR TRACKS

Why do some people break the law and hunt endangered animals?

African elephant

>>> ELEPHANTS, RHINOS, AND PANGOLINS ARE THREE VERY DIFFERENT ANIMALS, BUT THEY HAVE SOMETHING IN COMMON.

Their populations are in decline due to poaching. Why do hunters go after these creatures? Elephant tusks, rhino horns, and pangolin scales sell for high prices in some parts of the world. If people stopped buying these animal parts, the cycle would end.

The Trouble With Tusks

Elephants use their tusks to defend themselves, gather food, and dig water holes in times of drought. But their tusks also put the animals in great danger. For thousands of years, people have hunted elephants for their ivory tusks. Ivory has been used to make many items, from jewelry to piano keys. A few centuries ago, as many as 10 million elephants roamed Earth. Today, there are only a few hundred thousand.

Fortunately, ivory sales have been banned in most countries. Now it's up to governments to crack down on those who break the law.

Rhinos at Risk

Rhino horn is made of keratin, the same material found in fingernails. But in some places, it sells for more than the price of gold. The horn is ground up and used to make medicines. Scientists have long said these concoctions have no healing power, but that hasn't put an end to people seeking them out, particularly in China and Vietnam. The demand for rhino horn has taken a terrible toll on the animals. Unlike elephant tusks, rhino horns can grow back. But to save time and avoid getting injured or caught, poachers usually kill the animals before removing their horns. Experts say there were once about one million rhinos in the wild. Now fewer than 30,000 remain.

Protecting rhinos is far from simple. South Africa, which is home to most of the world's rhinos, tried ramping up security for the animals, but the poaching continued. So, conservationists came up with another plan—moving rhinos to low-poaching zones (see pages 186–187). Transporting two-ton (1.8-t) mammals hundreds of miles may sound extreme. But bringing rhinos to a safer place is one way to ensure that the animals will have a future.

The Struggle to Save the Pangolin

Many people know about the challenges facing elephants and rhinos. But fewer are aware of the plight of the pangolin. The scaly mammal lives in sub-Saharan Africa and Southeast Asia, and laps up insects with its long, sticky tongue. Pangolins are hunted for both their scales and their meat. In some parts of Asia, the smooth, brown scales are ground into powder and used to make remedies for various ailments. The scales are made of keratin, just like fingernails and rhino horns, and scientists say they have no curative powers. Yet many people are willing to pay top dollar for the supposed medicines. Trade in pangolin goods has been banned since 2016, but the scales and meat are still sold illegally in several places.

A HIGH PRICE TO PAY

One way to help elephants, rhinos, and pangolins: Never buy these animal products!

ANIMAL PART: Elephant tusks
USED FOR: Jewelry, trinkets, figurines, combs, chopsticks

ANIMAL PART: Pangolin scales
USED FOR: Remedies

ANIMAL PART: Rhino horn
USED FOR: Remedies

BACK FROM THE BRINK

After nearly going extinct, these creatures are making a comeback.

>>> **THESE THREE ANIMALS CAME DANGEROUSLY CLOSE TO BEING WIPED OFF THE PLANET.** But all three were saved thanks to the efforts of dedicated individuals. Here are their stories.

Baby mountain gorilla

Against All Odds

There was a time when it seemed that saving the mountain gorilla was a lost cause. In the 1980s, the subspecies was down to just a few hundred individuals—and their situation was dire. Much of their habitat had been replaced by farms. Poachers added to the problem. And when humans fought their own wars, the gorillas were often caught in the crossfire.

But a group of conservationists managed to turn the gorillas' situation around by setting up an around-the-clock system for monitoring and protecting the animals that remained. In 2018, a count revealed that the mountain gorilla population had climbed to 1,004, and the subspecies was upgraded from "critically endangered" to "endangered." Today, the gorillas are still far from being in the clear, but with the help of a dedicated team, their numbers are moving in the right direction.

Return of the Echo Parakeet

If you were to take a walk in a forest in Mauritius, you might see an emerald green parrot perched on the branch of a tree. Hundreds of these birds, known as echo parakeets, can now be found on the African island. But not too long ago, the birds seemed to be on a one-way path to extinction. Most had disappeared due to habitat loss and competition from species that had been brought to the island. By the 1980s, there were thought to be no more than 12 echo parakeets left.

That's when conservationists set out to save the species before it was too late. They trimmed tree branches to prevent hungry monkeys from reaching the birds' nests. They treated the nests with insecticides to keep away biting flies. During food shortages, they provided the birds with extra meals. And they raised dozens of chicks in captivity, later releasing them into the wild. By the end of 2015, there were 650 echo parakeets in the forest, and the birds' numbers have continued to rise.

Echo parakeet

A Second Chance

It's easy to see how the scimitar-horned oryx got its name. The antelope's horns are curved, much like the blade of a scimitar, a type of sword. The magnificent horns can grow to a length of four feet (1.2 m), making the oryx stand out even from a distance. Perhaps that's why the antelope was targeted by hunters. At one time, as many as a million of these animals roamed northern Africa's Sahel region. But in the 1980s, the species went extinct in the wild.

That sounds like the end of the oryx's story, but it's not. Before the antelope went extinct, many were taken into captivity at locations around the world. Conservationists hoped that, one day, the animals would be returned to the wild. In 2016, that wish came true. A group of 23 oryx were released into their natural habitat. Soon after, one of the animals gave birth to a little calf. It was the first wild member of the species to be born in nearly 30 years. Many more oryx have since joined the group, and the animals' spectacular horns can be seen on the Sahel once again.

Scimitar-horned oryx

Scimitar-horned oryx can tolerate an internal body temperature of about 116°F (47°C). This allows them to **AVOID SWEATING,** conserving water.

"We love getting down on the ground with these giants and getting this perspective. They are so impressive."
—Beverly and Dereck Joubert

179

LIVING WITH WILDLIFE

Creative solutions are helping humans live side by side with wild animals.

>>> **THERE ARE MORE THAN SEVEN AND A HALF BILLION PEOPLE ON EARTH, MORE THAN AT ANY OTHER TIME IN HISTORY.** So it's no surprise that humans are taking up more space than ever before—including wild space. Can people and wild animals live side by side in peace? These creative approaches suggest that sharing the planet is possible.

A Buzz-Worthy Approach

To farmers who make their livelihood in areas where elephants roam, the animals are a major cause for concern. Elephants have been known to raid crops, such as potatoes and corn, for food and to cause major property damage in the process. Sometimes, fed-up farmers resort to harming the animals.

To cut down on this conflict, researchers came up with a creative solution. Knowing that elephants are terrified of bees, they developed special fences containing multiple beehives, all linked together by wire. When an elephant touches the fence, the hives swing, and a swarm of angry bees comes flying out. The first fences were so successful at keeping elephants away from crops that the enclosures are now being used in several African countries.

A fence made of thorny acacia tree branches in Tanzania

Beehive fence in Kibale National Park, Uganda

Living Walls

In northern Tanzania, where the Maasai people live and raise their cattle, conflict between humans and lions is nothing new. But with the lions' habitat shrinking and their natural prey disappearing, the cats have been turning up on Maasai farms more often than in the past. When the big cats go after livestock instead of wild prey, people are understandably angry—and in some cases, they retaliate by killing the lions. But a low-tech solution is putting an end to the cycle.

Tall enclosures made of trees encircled with chain-link fences have been installed at more than 1,000 farms. These "living walls" protect livestock from lions around the clock. With their cattle secure, herders can sleep soundly at night—and they no longer have reason to go after lions. It is one case in which good fences truly do make good neighbors.

All Bark and No Bite

Over the last century, cheetah numbers have plummeted throughout Africa. The country of Namibia has been no exception. One reason: Farmers were killing cheetahs to protect their livestock. Today, however, much of the killing has stopped. How? A group called the Cheetah Conservation Fund brought in dogs called Anatolian shepherds to guard the cattle. These dogs have successfully protected livestock in Turkey for thousands of years. Now they are doing the same in Namibia. When cheetahs approach farms, the dogs make a racket, disrupting the cats' quiet ambush hunting technique. Cheetahs stay away, and they also stay safe.

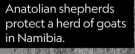

Anatolian shepherds protect a herd of goats in Namibia.

CONSERVATION HEROES

These individuals have dedicated their lives to restoring and protecting Africa's wildlife.

A Madagascan big-headed turtle basks on a log in Madagascar.

>>> **PEOPLE WHO GIVE THEIR ALL TO SAVING ANIMALS ARE RARELY REWARDED WITH FORTUNE OR FAME.** Those who pursue careers in conservation do so simply because they care—about wildlife, about communities, and about the future of our planet. Each of these heroes is proof of the difference one person can make.

Turning the Tide for Turtles

When Juliette Velosoa took on the cause of Madagascar's side-necked turtles in 1998, the reptiles were in serious trouble. The turtles' freshwater habitat was in decline, and the animals were being overhunted. Velosoa knew that to save the rare turtles, called the rere (pronounced ray-ray), in Madagascar, she would need the support of local communities. She recruited villagers to guard the turtles' nests and help improve the quality of their habitat by keeping the water clean and making sure not to remove too many fish. Velosoa got kids and adults alike excited about protecting their country's only freshwater turtle.

Velosoa and her team also boosted the turtles' population through a "head-starting" effort. To give the animals a better chance of survival, they raised hundreds of hatchlings in captivity and released them into the wild only once they were strong enough to stand a chance against predators.

Gray-crowned crane

Doctor Crane

When Olivier Nsengimana was a boy growing up in Rwanda, he did not have access to TV or comic books. He has said that instead of Spider-Man and Superman, the magnificent gray-crowned cranes that he saw in the forest were his superheroes. Now a veterinarian, Nsengimana is working to save the birds he has always admired.

A gray-crowned crane is a large bird that stands out thanks to its headdress of golden feathers. The eye-catching crane is considered to be a symbol of good luck—a belief that has led to the bird's decline. Many have been snatched from the wild and brought into homes and hotels for display. The cranes have also suffered due to habitat loss.

Olivier Nsengimana

To combat the many threats affecting gray-crowned cranes, Nsengimana and his team are taking a multipronged approach. They are returning captive cranes to the wild, educating local communities about what they can do to help, and planting hundreds of trees to restore the forest. Nsengimana can't fly, but he is precisely the type of superhero the cranes need.

Forest Focused

In Tanzania, where Makala Jasper grew up, trees are often used for fuel or removed to make room for farmland. Jasper worried about the wild animals that rely on the forest.

After training to become a scientist, he returned home with a plan. He knew that Tanzania's coastal forests contain some of the most valuable trees in the world. The wood of the mpingo tree, also known as African blackwood, is the best material for making woodwind instruments, such as clarinets and oboes. Jasper taught local communities how to keep their forests healthy by cutting down a safe number of trees and growing plenty of new ones. With Jasper's help, the communities have earned hundreds of thousands of dollars from timber sales while sustaining their forests, too.

Makala Jasper

WHAT YOU CAN DO

Here's how you can be an ally to endangered animals.

>>> **YOU DON'T NEED TO LIVE AMONG ELEPHANTS AND RHINOS TO HELP THEM.** There are steps you can take to support endangered animals, wherever you are. Check out three ideas for befriending the creatures that need you the most.

A naturalist talks to children about the animals at Potomac Overlook Park, Arlington, Virginia, U.S.A.

Speak Up

Find out how government policies are impacting endangered species. If there is something that you think needs to change, write a letter to lawmakers, sharing your point of view. You can also spread the word about an issue by creating a petition and asking others to sign it. The more you raise your voice, the more your message will be heard!

Become an Expert

Do you want to learn more about an animal featured in this book? Go for it! Visit a zoo or a wildlife sanctuary to see your favorite creature in action. Check out books from the library. With a parent or guardian's permission, do research online. Then, share your knowledge by creating your own pamphlet, book, or website. Your dedication, along with the information you pass along, will inspire your friends and family to care more about endangered animals, too.

Lend a Hand

With a parent or guardian's help, find a conservation group whose work you'd like to support. If the group holds events in your area, you can volunteer to help out. You can also support an organization's work by holding a fundraiser. Some kids have raised money for endangered species by selling origami rhinos, elephant-shaped cookies, and paintings of animals. What creative ideas do you have?

Volunteers help clean up a public beach in San Francisco, California, U.S.A.

MAKE EARTH-FRIENDLY CHOICES

Animals are counting on us to take care of the planet. What can you do to help the environment? Here are four tips.
- Help keep outside spaces in your community litter free. Participate in cleanup days at beaches or parks.
- Recycle. Make sure you know all the rules. In some towns, all recyclables can be placed in one container. Other communities require sorting.
- Avoid drinking bottled water. Use a reusable bottle instead.
- Whenever possible, walk, ride a bike, or take public transportation instead of taking a car.

A FRIEND TO ELEPHANTS

Téa Megill of Hawaii was 10 when she found out about the challenges facing elephants—and she decided to take action. She set up a lemonade stand to raise funds in support of the gentle giants. She got permission to move her stand into the Honolulu Zoo, and she started making bracelets and tote bags to sell, too. Every Wednesday, Téa sets up shop at the zoo. When visitors stop by her stand, she takes the opportunity to tell them why elephants need their help. Téa's efforts show that you don't have to be an adult to make an elephant-size difference.

Téa Megill

JOURNEY WITH THE JOUBERTS

RHINO RESCUE

FOR YEARS, WE'D THOUGHT OF OURSELVES FIRST AND FOREMOST AS BIG-CAT PEOPLE. Lions, cheetahs, and leopards had long been at the center of our conservation work. But in 2015, we found out that rhinos were in terrible trouble. The animals were being targeted for their horns, which can fetch high sums in certain parts of the world. Poachers were killing them at a rate of one every seven and a half hours. When we learned just how dire the situation had become, our first thought was: What can we do?

We scratched our heads and came up with a bold plan. We would remove rhinos from high-poaching zones and place them in an area where they would be protected. We knew just the place to move them to: Botswana. The country's government had devoted vast resources, including the support of the military, to stomp out poaching. These efforts had worked, and elephants were thriving there. With our help, rhinos could join them.

We set out to transport 100 rhinos. Moving a two-ton (1.8-t) beast hundreds of miles is no small feat. We needed a team of experts. We needed access to helicopters and planes. And of course, we needed the funds to make it all happen. It turned out that many people wanted to help. Even the youngest conservationists found a way to lend a hand. Children in South Africa folded hundreds of origami rhinos and sold them to raise money for the program. By 2017, all the pieces of our plan had come together, and we brought our first group of rhinos to Botswana. Watching the animals munch on grass in their new home filled us with hope.

We've now transported 87 rhinos, and each one has arrived in Botswana safe and sound. What's more, they are growing in numbers. Since the start of the program, 50 calves have been born. When one of those little rhinos arrived in March 2017, Beverly was recovering from an injury and could not be in the field with the rest of the team. The people who monitor the rhinos named the baby Beverly. So today, a plump little rhino runs around Botswana with Beverly's name. It is our wish that, one day, she and her fellow rhinos will no longer need our help to survive.

INDEX

Boldface indicates illustrations.

INDEX

CREDITS

Since 1888, the National Geographic Society has funded more than 12,000 research, exploration,
and preservation projects around the world. The Society receives funds from National Geographic Partners, LLC,
funded in part by your purchase. A portion of the proceeds from this book supports
this vital work. To learn more, visit natgeo.com/info.

For more information, visit nationalgeographic.com,
call 1-877-873-6846, or write to the following address:

National Geographic Partners, LLC
1145 17th Street N.W.
Washington, DC 20036-4688 U.S.A.

For librarians and teachers: nationalgeographic.com/books/librarians-and-educators

More for kids from National Geographic: natgeokids.com

National Geographic Kids magazine inspires children to explore their world with fun
yet educational articles on animals, science, nature, and more. Using fresh storytelling and
amazing photography, *Nat Geo Kids* shows kids ages 6 to 14 the fascinating truth about the world—and
why they should care. kids.nationalgeographic.com/subscribe

For rights or permissions inquiries, please contact National Geographic Books Subsidiary Rights:
bookrights@natgeo.com

Designed by Julide Dengel and Shannon Palatta

The publisher would like to thank the following people for help bringing this book to life:
Ariane Szu-Tu, editor; Grace Hill Smith, project manager; Amanda Larsen, design director; Julide Dengel,
designer; Lori Epstein, photo director; and Anne LeongSon and Gus Tello, design production assistants.

Hardcover ISBN: 978-1-4263-7187-5
Reinforced library binding ISBN: 978-1-4263-7188-2

Printed in Hong Kong
21/PPHK/1

Peter Paul and Mary

——————— ‹•› ———————

DEDICATED TO
MARY TRAVERS AND PETE SEEGER

FIFTY YEARS

IN MUSIC AND LIFE

BY PETER YARROW, NOEL PAUL STOOKEY & MARY TRAVERS

A NOTE OF THANKS TO THE PHOTOGRAPHERS:

Thank all of you wonderful photographers, identified or not, who made this book possible. It's been a labor of love and, we believe, truly shares the heart of what the experience of the trio has been. After doing an extensive search to find their origin, we included some photographs for which the photographer could not be identified. They help tell the story of our lives and career together and, on balance, we thought that the photographers, most of whom had become personal friends of the trio, would be pleased to have their work represented in our book. Nonetheless, we very much wish to hear from anyone who knows, or who thinks they know, the names and/or addresses of the unidentified photographers so we can thank them, credit them in later editions, give them a hug (virtual or in person) and offer them a proper use fee. Please contact by email at photoinfo@peterpaulandmary.com.

Text copyright © 2015 Peter, Paul and Mary
Image copyrights held by the individuals listed on page 144

Charlesbridge and colophon are registered trademarks of Charlesbridge Publishing, Inc.

An Imagine Book
Published by Charlesbridge
85 Main Street
Watertown, MA 02472
(617) 926-0329
www.charlesbridge.com

Peter, Paul, and Mary (Musical group), author.
Peter, Paul, and Mary : fifty years in music and life / Peter, Paul & Mary ;
foreword by John F. Kerry, US Secretary of State.
     pages cm
 ISBN 978-1-936140-32-9 (hardback)
1. Peter, Paul, and Mary (Musical group) 2. Folk singers--United
States--Biography. I. Kerry, John, 1943- writer of supplementary textual
content. II. Title.
ML421.P485P48 2014
782.42162'1300922--dc23
[B]
                         2014014187

Printed in China. Manufactured in December, 2014.

10 9 8 7 6 5 4 3 2

ISBN: 978-1-936140-32-9

For information about custom editions, special sales, premium and corporate purchases,
please contact Charlesbridge Publishing at specialsales@charlesbridge.com

CONTENTS

FOREWORD

I was a college kid on a cold Connecticut night in 1964 when I first heard Mary's angelic alto. On that night in New Haven and on so many nights over the next five decades, in so many places all over the world, Peter, Paul and Mary's music asked more of us than to simply sing along. "The hammer of justice" and "the bell of freedom!" These are more than just lyrics; they were then, and they remain, a call to conscience, and as Peter especially has always reminded me, when something pulls at your conscience, you need to act.

As Peter, Paul and Mary journeyed from coffeehouses and campuses to the Billboard Top 40, there could be no doubt that we were all living in turbulent times. But in their harmonies was a magic and message more powerful than a decade of discord and exhilaration.

That is why, after all these years, we return to the music. That is why when we turn the pages of this incredible book, we are questioned, liberated, and challenged once again.

I know my experience with Peter, Paul and Mary is one that I shared with so many in those years of challenge and transformation. Their music became an anchor: "Blowin' in the Wind" as the war in Vietnam escalated. "Leavin' on a Jet Plane" as I left to join the war. "Puff, the Magic Dragon" as I patrolled the Mekong Delta. Their songs became the soundtrack of my life and of a generation.

They changed the cultural fabric of this nation forever. Peter, Paul and Mary brought folk music from the shadows of the McCarthy blacklist era to the living rooms and radio stations of every town in America. They gave the world its first listen to young songwriting talents from Bob Dylan to John Denver, Gordon Lightfoot to Laura Nyro.

And though their music might stop and the band would break up for years, they never stopped marching. They marched for peace, for racial justice, for workers' rights. They marched against gun violence, homelessness, and world hunger. They marched for clean air and clean water, against apartheid and nuclear proliferation.

Through both their songs and their struggle, they helped propel our nation on its greatest journey, on the march toward greater equality. With their passion and persistence, Peter, Paul and Mary helped widen the circle of our democracy.

It was at Dr. King's March on Washington, that Peter, Paul and Mary first performed "Blowin' in the Wind." On that day and for decades thereafter, they made it clear that it was up to all of us to reach for the answer by reaching out to one another and to the world. Their message was not defined by protest but by taking responsibility—taking the risks that peace, the most powerful answer of all, always requires.

After the 1960s, those risks left many of us with wounds and battle scars, physical and spiritual, real and metaphorical. We saw too many of our heroes and friends—our flowers—gone to graveyards far too soon. In the years to come, their music helped us to heal.

It was in 1971, at one of the many marches in Washington that Peter, Paul and Mary helped to lead, when I first met Mary. She once told me she was always guided by advice she got from her mother: "Be careful of compromise," she said. "There's a very thin line between compromise and accomplice." She wasn't just speaking about music or even politics. It was a worldview, a philosophy of life—and it is within these pages and in the spirit that Peter and Noel (Paul) continue to share with audiences around the world, Mary's spirit endures.

But this book is not a tribute to any "time that was," or even to three incredible people who changed music and our lives forever. Instead, it is a testament to what they achieved with their audience, both as musicians and as individuals, as artists and as activists, as Americans and as citizens of the world.

It is also a testament to what's left undone. The questions that Peter, Paul and Mary posed more than fifty years ago at the March on Washington—how many roads, how many years will it take?—these are still our questions and we still have a responsibility to answer.

That is why the power of Peter, Paul and Mary's music and their work in the world is enduring. That is why it remains an inspiration for the work to come, for our work together, and for all we hope to leave behind.

One of my favorite Peter, Paul and Mary songs has always been "Sweet Survivor." I was moved when Mary sang it for me on my fiftieth birthday, and then when Peter sang it for me on a cold bus in Iowa in 2003. Its words still speak to the future, not the past:

> Carry on my sweet survivor, carry on my lonely friend.
> Don't give up on the dream, and don't let it end.
> Carry on my sweet survivor, you've carried it so long.
> So may it come again, carry on, carry on, carry on.

And so as we read this book—and remember the music—we do it with much more than nostalgia: we do it because Peter, Paul and Mary remind us still to carry on.

John F. Kerry
US Secretary of State

PREFACE

Through this book, we wanted to tell the visual story, and create an accompanying narrative, that could provide an in-depth sense of what Peter, Paul and Mary stood for, lived, and shared. *Peter, Paul and Mary: Fifty Years in Music and Life* presents the arc of the trio's fifty-year association, as well as a glimpse of the crucible of change and progress that the country experienced in the decades we shared together.

We are grateful to see our journey captured in remarkable images that were taken by so many superbly gifted photographers, as well as some talented friends who, as amateurs, captured some of our more private moments with great taste and sensitivity.

The story that winds through these images offers a candid look at what we were feeling and experiencing at a time in which we found ourselves in the eye of the storm. These times witnessed a mighty struggle, emanating mainly from grassroots, ordinary citizens, rather than from a top-down effort, to remedy some of the most egregious failures of our society and move us toward greater justice and, we dearly hoped, peace.

Through our music, our appearances at demonstrations, and, in fact, at every concert, we tried to share and contribute to the ardent messages of folk singers and writers who had come before us and who had inspired previous generations in earlier struggles.

All three of our voices created the narrative of this book. You will not know who wrote what, but as in our music, you will know that what finally emerged is the distillation of a group process that characterized the way we decided on the causes we chose to pursue, the choices of our songs, and the creation of their arrangements.

We agreed right from the start that our musical efforts and social-political advocacies had to be agreed upon unanimously. Any one of us could say no, which could be maddening at times; however, this agreement kept us honest, on an equal footing, and compelled us to find a way to agree. In retrospect, the results were better and truer to ourselves than what we might have come to without this agreement. Consensus, it was called, and consensus it still is—and that is the way this book was created.

Noel and Peter's words have been merged, revised, and revised again, to create this book's narrative. Mary's words and perspective—drawn from her writings, interviews, and conversations—were, more than anything, curated and represented by her great friend, yet another strong woman, our manager, Martha Hertzberg, who also became the book's photo editor, a task that compelled her to sift through hundreds and hundreds of photographs to create the visual story line.

The credit for conceiving *Peter, Paul and Mary: Fifty Years in Music and Life* belongs to Charlie Nurnberg, one of the most respected, prolific, and creative publishers in the business. Charlie knows how to insist on a standard of quality that accompanies the books he publishes, and, gratefully, he also affords his fellow creators the kind of respect that allows their imaginations and creativity to run free.

The design of this book is the work of a dear friend of the trio, Maria Villar, who has worked with us on many projects including our retrospective box set, and has become our "go to" person when we need the skill of a gifted graphic designer, especially so during this last decade of our career.

Charlie Nurnberg chose Dawn Cusick to be the editor of the reams of writing that had to be collated and crafted into a coherent story that accompanies the photographs. Dawn's editorial skills, combined with her deep regard for the trio's history, is greatly appreciated, as well as her personal embrace of what we sought to achieve.

Finally, there is the startlingly moving introduction written by our dear friend and ally for the majority of our career, US Secretary of State John F. Kerry. John comes from a place of deep solidarity of spirit, great personal friendship, and mutual affection forged over many decades. In November of 2009, John's words catalyzed Mary's memorial with their love, irony, and humor in a tribute of tributes, and here in his foreword, celebrating the trio's fifty years together, he honors us once again. John's words pay Peter, Paul and Mary as great a compliment as we have ever received. His words humble us.

One could not ask for more caring and wonderful partners to help create this book's retelling of the many years the trio spent together.

With all our gratitude,
Peter, Paul and Mary

When we first sat down to sing in the grungy, fifth-floor East Village walk-up where Tom Paxton and Noel Paul Stookey shared a loft space, there was magic in the air. We had chosen the nursery rhyme "Mary Had a Little Lamb" to test the personal and sonic chemistry of our voices. Each time we switched leads, our voices came to life with new and wonderful textures and coloration. It was undeniable: the magic enveloped us.

We called Albert Grossman, Peter's manager at the time, who was eagerly awaiting word. Breathlessly, Peter told him, "This is it." Generally regarded as a genius of sorts (a well-earned title), Albert had conceived of the group and, along with Peter, he brought the trio together. Because our first meeting was so inspiring, we started rehearsing the very next day. We met in Mary's tiny apartment, a fourth-floor walk-up that was at the center of the action in Greenwich Village, on the famous MacDougal Street. The apartment was so small that, literally, we could not sit down in three chairs without a major furniture rearrangement.

Having grown up in the Village, Mary was one of its most notable and admired denizens. A single mother of twenty-three and recently separated from her writer husband, Mary was on "mommy duty," as we called it, most of the day caring for one-year-old Erika, so we needed to meet at her apartment. Our rehearsals, it turned out, lasted for seven straight months, at which time we were reasonably "tight" (we could sing well together) and had enough songs to begin performing. We usually worked all day, creating arrangements with our new music director, Milt Okun, starting with songs such as "The Cruel War," "This Train," "Where Have All the Flowers Gone," and "500 Miles."

None of us had any money. At the time, Peter was performing at a coffeehouse called The Café Wha?, a moderately delightful dungeon that is still open today. He owned one pair of green corduroy pants that he wore virtually every day, by necessity. Noel was the least impoverished of the trio because he performed and ran the entertainment at the Gaslight, one of the top coffeehouses on MacDougal Street. Coffeehouse performers' sole earnings came from their share of the money put in the hat that was passed around after each set. Noel's performing at a "top" coffeehouse meant that, at the end of the night, there was a bit more to share among four or five performers.

In addition to being a singer and guitarist with roots in classical music, jazz, and pop, Noel was a Village comic along with fellow coffeehouse comedians such as Woody Allen and Bill Cosby (Cos). Noel's humor used sound effects in ways similar to the iconic Jonathan Winters's "out there" routines. At the time, being "out there" was a compliment, and Winters was one of the most admired "sick comedians" of the day. Noel's vignettes were unlike anyone else's because they boasted more than humor. His routines characterized real, middle-American folks, providing a looking glass that gently jibed at the foolishness of contemporary cultural rituals such as teenage drag racing.

The trio's manager, Albert Grossman, was a powerful figure in the 1960s' Greenwich Village folk era. A dyed-in-the-wool iconoclast from Chicago's cutting-edge creative scene, Albert was noted for, among other things, his desire to work with artists who would break the mold of what was expected. In describing his concept for a trio to Peter, an idea that Albert had carried for some years before our birth, he said he was looking for a unique chemistry of voices that included, in his words, a strong woman singer, a gifted comedic performer (who could also sing), and someone, like Peter, who was a heartfelt, tasteful singer of folk songs. Bingo!

Right: The trio in Greenwich Village near the iconic Circle in the Square Theatre circa 1962

The trio during an early 1960s' television appearance on *PM East* hosted by Mike Wallace

In the early '60s, those of us who shared the Village's crucible of creativity looked at ourselves with fresh eyes, listened to one another with fresh ears, and invented new words and phrases to describe our feelings. (The phrases *uptight* [anxious], *dig yourself* [be aware of your absurdity], and *get behind* [adopt or agree with a point of view] come to mind.) The world was changing fast, and new ideas and traditions were forming around what was important, truthful, honest, and worth pursuing in life. Through our music, our trio became part of an unprecedented exploration, creating a new—sometimes loving, sometimes defiant—language of feelings that we shared in song. For the moment, money didn't matter, things didn't matter, and security didn't matter. We were healthy, young, and filled with the intoxication of

Shel Silverstein, a good friend of the trio, was a Renaissance guy of many talents, but few know that besides being a brilliant writer, songwriter, and children's illustrator/author, he once performed at coffeehouses. Around 1963, the trio played Chicago's Gate of Horn, the famous folk club, and Shel was our opening act. He was very funny and wondrously odd, and he captured us better than anyone (note Mary's stance) in this caricature that he drew on a napkin after the show and gave to us as a gift.

Above: The trio sings on the set of one of their first television shows in the early 1960s.
Opposite page: Mary sits front and center with "the boys" (as she fondly called Noel and Peter) playing in the background during an early photo session. During photo shoots, it was common for us to sing at first to find our closeness. Then we would stay in position, mouths not moving, while the photo was taken.

the Village, which gave us a cloak of invulnerability. Love was in the air, and new songs, ideas, and emotions were giving birth to new ways of viewing the world that would reshape our destinies as individuals and as a society. As Mary described those days, "For me, Peter, Paul and Mary was a project. Everyone in the Village had one—it was their identity. The waitress was an actress; the espresso operator, a writer; the bus boy, a painter. So, Peter, Paul and Mary became my project."

We sang to the audience, of course, but just as frequently, we sang to one another. Each song was a series of improvisational surprises, and we could sense the audience joining us in these explorations. From night to night, songs varied in their nuanced meanings and the way they were delivered. In one concert, "Where Have All the Flowers Gone" was defiant; in another, sorrowful; in yet another, it was a blend of pain and disbelief at the futility of war. During the anti–Vietnam War period, the tragedy of war and the despair over the fragmenting of our country's spirit was embedded in many of our songs.

Oddly, in the mid '60s, *Playboy* magazine accepted the public's nomination of Peter, Paul and Mary in its highly esteemed Playboy Jazz Poll. Even more oddly, the trio won Best Vocal Group (though folk is far from being jazz), and *Playboy* published this photo of us taken when we were recording.

The genuine laughter we often enjoyed nurtured us throughout the years. We shared a common sense of humor, and were a great audience for one another. We saw the world as comical and delightful, yet also painfully faulted and cruel at times. This was our balance, and sharing these emotions and views made us very close (and vulnerable) to one another. As with all people, we had our limits, and we learned to give each other space when we needed to be left alone.

Other than traditional folk songs, most of our early music was written by new writers who had inherited the heart of the folk tradition and created new ways of carrying on these traditions: Bob Dylan, Gordon Lightfoot, John Denver, and Laura Nyro, to name a few. Mary and Peter had learned our folk repertoire through the works of Pete Seeger, Woody Guthrie, The Weavers, Josh White, Burl Ives, and others. Noel was not a "folkie" by background, but he was an eager and willing entrant to the folk circle. Finding songs that respected and retained the legacy of traditional folk artists was important to us. We felt our songs needed to be arranged and performed in ways that honored our inherited tradition. Of the songs we wrote ourselves, Noel and Peter did most of the writing. Mary was the poet in the group, and her poems were set to music on a few occasions.

Above: The trio rides on one of San Francisco's famous cable cars during our first West Coast gig at the renowned folk club, the Hungry "I," in 1962. During this trip, our first single, "Lemon Tree," broke out.

Right: Frequent travel requires careful packing. In our trio, Noel was by far the most gifted packer of our rented station wagon trunks. The fragile double bass would have to be fit in with the guitars and our bags, which was tricky. In the early years of touring, we would sometimes drive, sleep, and perform day, after day, after day. But who cared?—it was a blast.

Songs under consideration had to be embraced by everyone if we were to incorporate them into our repertoire, and some of our trio's biggest debates revolved around a song's lyrics. When one of us had a philosophical problem with a lyric, that person lobbied for specific additions or deletions. (If the changes were significant, and someone outside the group had written the song, we would contact her or him for permission to make alterations.) One song that became the subject of passionate analysis and discussion was Bob Dylan's "The Times They Are a-Changin'." As the lead singer for this song, Mary called the ultimate shots on most aspects of its arrangement and presentation because the success and validity of a song's performance rested on her shoulders. In one of her solo lines, "Come mothers and fathers throughout the land, and don't criticize what you don't understand," Mary wanted to change the word *don't* to *can't,* reflecting her belief that adults and parents were not being dense—they simply were not able to grasp what was happening in the lives and new perspectives of their children. Mary's version was gentler in its implications, and we always sang it her way.

Sometimes, even love songs or personal songs such as "500 Miles" became a vehicle for us to express—sometimes subtly—how deeply we yearned to be a moral nation. In the late '60s, we came to oppose the war, against which we marched many times. Our hearts, with both love and despair, went out to our returning Vietnam veterans, particularly those who were wounded, and later to those demoralized by their traumatizing experiences and memories. These times were complicated and

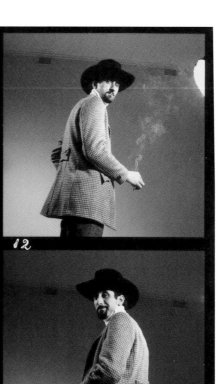

challenging for us—and for our nation—and our songs often revealed our personal heartache. The tradition of folk music had taken hold of our beings, showing us the path to sharing all that we feared, abominated, hoped for, and cared about. We not only sang the songs, but we also did our best to live their messages, advocating and demonstrating in word and song, as Pete Seeger and The Weavers had shown us through their inspiring example.

A 1963 photo session captures the trio trying on evolving personas. Noel was stylish and cool. Peter was playful but also "the serious one," predicting his future polarities. Mary vacillated between shyly considering the fact that she was beautiful in other people's eyes and starting to believe in herself as the strong and insightful women's role model she was becoming.

Above: This photograph captures our momentary pause right before switching from the normal folk version of "Old Blue" to the rock and roll spoof version. We would turn our heads away from the audience, and then spin around and launch into a hysteria-tinged version of the song that Noel intoned had been altered by a "nasty, unscrupulous modifier." The parody was our first group comedy piece, and came from Peter's solo set before the trio formed.

Left: It was our habit to run onstage holding one another's hands. No one ever told us to do this; it just happened. A joyful entrance and a sign of our togetherness, we literally "hit the stage running."

Each night, we sang songs that had been handed down to us by traditional, old-timey blues singers such as Reverend Gary Davis and Brother John Sellers and no-frills traditional folk-country singers such as Jean Ritchie. Some of the most remarkable gifts we received were the songs we learned from the more recent keepers of the flame, such as Josh White, and our role model, Pete Seeger. (Privately, Mary called us Seeger's Raiders.) We knew, of course, that Pete and the other members of The Weavers would have ignited a folk renaissance a decade earlier if Senator Joe McCarthy's "witch hunt" had not tragically ended their career by blacklisting them. The blacklist destroyed their career by preventing them from working in any established performing venue. Pete played many a summer camp to make ends meet, teaching and inspiring a new generation of folk singers and activists that was soon to become the '60s' Folk Renaissance. Ironically, performing this way amplified Pete's presence on the folk scene, but the price he and the other members of The Weavers paid was a bitter one that none of us from the '60s ever forgot.

Silliness and fun emerge from Noel's amazing gifts as a comedian. Noel didn't have to try to be funny; he just was. When he became one of his sweet and sincere-but-unaware characters, Mary and Peter couldn't help themselves. They would just crack up.

For us, recording was a very serious process. In those days, each twelve-song album told the story of what was on our minds at the time, and explored our thoughts and feelings about where our collective lives were taking us. On average, we recorded one song per three-hour session. We'd sing a song in its entirety, critique it on its first playback, and then record it again, and again, and again. The aim was to record until the performance peaked. Then we'd stop. This process meant that we sometimes did a huge number of takes, sometimes as many as fifteen or twenty. The discipline and concentration often challenged our patience, which tended to wear thin after the first two hours. There was no "over-dubbing" in those days, no chance to add a new instrument or change a vocal. We recorded on just three tracks, whereas now, an infinite number of tracks can be added at will. At the time, you had to live with what you created, live, on the spot, which was, in retrospect, a blessing that made for authentic, exceedingly "present" renditions.

Some of our most wonderful moments as a trio took place in the recording studio, often during the playbacks when we were startled to hear the sounds that the recording engineer had created. By common agreement, we showed our respect for the engineer's work by listening in silence until a playback finished. Only then did we voice an opinion.

We were left to create in our own way, and at our own pace, in the studio. As with very few other artists, we had no "suits" (record company execs) at our recording sessions. Our manager Albert had lobbied for, and brilliantly crafted, a contract stipulating that we had the right to be the sole arbiters of song selection and recording methodology, a privilege that was not extended to most artists at the time. Albert set the stage for a music industry change that would soon deeply affect the careers

Above and opposite page: Recording is an intense and exciting challenge, and very different from singing onstage. For us, the positioning of the mics in a tight triangle heightened the intimacy of the recording studio. We always looked directly at one another during the entire take, sensing the developing drama of the song. We were both performer and audience to one another and, in both capacities, we knew when we were sailing.

of other artists he managed: Richie Havens, Gordon Lightfoot, Bob Dylan, and Janis Joplin. They were all, famously and blessedly, left alone to create without corporate oversight.

For our first four albums, our engineer was the extraordinarily talented, and now legendary, Bill Schwartau, who mentored the soon-to-be equally iconic Phil Ramone. Almost a decade later, Phil became our engineer/producer, a task he shared with our musical director, Milt Okun. On our first albums, we were thrilled by the sounds Bill created just by choosing exactly the right microphones and just the right type of echo (now sometimes called reverb). "Outboard"

The rehearsals during which we created our parts for song arrangements required focused and exacting work. In our first decade together, Milt Okun (top left) was our soft-spoken musical director and creative partner. His contributions were many—sometimes suggesting parts, sometimes refereeing, and always keeping the lid on the inevitable fatigue and impatience that, after four solid hours, would creep into the room like a gremlin.

(additional equipment to shape a sound) had yet to be invented. Importantly, Albert directed Bill to physically separate our voices and guitars so that one voice would be on the left with its guitar (generally Noel), one of us on the right with another guitar (generally Peter), and Mary would be in the center with the bass, which Bill Lee (father of Spike Lee) beautifully and melodically played as the fourth voice. Bruce Langhorne, with his cutting-edge and highly individualistic guitar "licks," accompanied us on many of the songs. The net result of the left-right separation was the uncommon nakedness of our voices. This unique sound was unheard of in the recordings of earlier vocal groups. Their voices were generally clumped in the center, which created a collective, somewhat anonymous, sound. On our recordings, each voice could be heard with full clarity, with all of its flaws, personality, and emotion fully exposed. This choice was one of the great gifts of our "manager to end all managers," Albert Grossman.

During songs such as "Where Have All the Flowers Gone," we often traveled a slender wire, hovering between great sadness and an almost divine sense of release.

Above: Mary endures the rigors of travel by reading; one book a day was her norm.
Above right: Noel and Peter play a game with Mary's daughter Erika, then age two. When we first toured, Erika came with us, and we delighted in entertaining her.

Developing songs for new albums kept our concert repertoire fresh, and helped us to grow artistically. More often than not, creating a song arrangement that truly satisfied us involved meticulous, focused, and repetitive work. The final result emerged from constant experimentation with numberless spontaneous tryouts of ideas suggested by each of us, until, in our collective assessment, the song finally worked. We shared a mutual delight and joy of accomplishment when a song fell into place. The result, we felt, truly belonged to us. Only then could we devote ourselves to interpreting the emotions and nuances that let the song tell its story. Once an arrangement was finalized, the song needed to percolate on stage, or mature, until the mechanics of performing it became automatic. Then we could devote ourselves to letting a new song live each night as its own creation with its own special interpretation, similar to, but different from, any other rendition. This process kept our songs fresh and our enthusiasm for singing them undiminished, despite the fact that many of our songs were performed hundreds, if not thousands, of times.

The trio rushes onstage, hand in hand. We always came onstage this way, sometimes running right through the audience.

Above and right: When we were first becoming famous, the *Saturday Evening Post* did an article on folk music and asked us to pose with a dog, honoring our silly spoof on "Old Blue," and also along-side a lemon tree to recognize our first single, "Lemon Tree." The newfound fame was fun and excit-ing, but in some ways it was strange and uncomfortable. How could we combine this superficiality with the grassroots spirit of the songs we were singing? That was something we had yet to sort out.

Bob Dylan's writing unquestionably brought the field of folk music, and folk-derived music, to a totally new level. When our shared manager, Albert Grossman, brought copies of Bobby's new reference "dubs" (quick recordings made at his publishing company) of his freshly written songs to a PP&M meeting in early 1963, we had an animated discussion about which songs we should consider. We all loved "Don't Think Twice," but we were overwhelmed by the remarkable and powerful ways "Blowin' in the Wind" spoke to the social/political movements of our time. Peter came to our next rehearsal with a suggested vocal arrangement that emphasized the song's dramatic urgency. For the first and only time in our careers, rather than wait for our next album, we went straight into the studio, recorded it, and immediately released it as a single that quickly climbed the pop charts. More important than sales, though, the song became a part of changing the emphasis of pop-charted music from "moon, spoon, June" lyrics to messages that spoke to America's conscience, and its dreams.

Bobby described his new album to Noel as, "Just me and the guitar and some new songs." When Noel asked him if he was happy with it, he talked about the mechanics and limitations of recording. He summarized his overall satisfaction with this memorable line: "It makes noise when you play it, though."

"Blowin' in the Wind" and "If I Had a Hammer" were two of the early, so-called "protest songs," although we saw them more as songs that affirmed our commitment to proposing answers, not just criticizing situations. "Blowin' in the Wind" was a lifelong favorite of Mary's, and she described the connection between the song and the Civil Rights Movement in an *Off the Record* interview with Joe Smith this way: "If I had to pick one song, my softest spot, it would be 'Blowin' in the Wind.' If you could imagine the March on Washington with Martin Luther King and singing that song in front of a quarter of a million people, black and white, who believed they could make America more generous and compassionate in a nonviolent way, you begin to know how incredible that belief was."

Though most people know that Dr. Martin Luther King Jr.'s "I Have a Dream" speech took place in Washington, DC, in 1963, few realize that his historic speech, as well as the music and introductions that preceded and followed it, were previously shared in a full rehearsal that took place in front of the marchers at the starting point, just a few hours prior to the march. One of the best-known photographs of our participation that day shows the Washington Monument in the distance behind a sea of people and press gathered before a stage roughly constructed for the run-through.

The march from this first gathering to the actual site of Dr. King's speech was solemn, dignified, moving, and purposeful, and not least because, after hearing Dr. King's amazing speech, we knew, we'd heard, and we were resolved. We walked, tens of people wide and thousands of people long, to the Lincoln Memorial, where Dr. King delivered what Mary

called "palpable hope." As for our participation,
we were three young people in our twenties who
had known popularity for less than two years, but
when we sang "Blowin' in the Wind" and "If I Had a
Hammer" that day, it changed the way we saw the
world . . . and our role in it.

The trio performs on the steps of the Lincoln Memorial during the March
on Washington for Jobs and Freedom, Washington, DC, August 28, 1963.

Visually, when we sang together, it was Mary who commanded the stage. Albert used to say that when people first attended a PP&M concert, all they could see or hear was Mary's performance. In many ways, he was right. Mary's stage presence and her dramatic beauty were as arresting as her remarkably expressive and powerful voice. As she moved, the folds of her stage dresses—her "costumes," as she called them—and the flips of her culture-changing hairstyle accentuated what she was feeling. Mary avoided the dance moves common to so many female performers of the time. Instead, her movements were direct responses to her emotions, and were never choreographed. Sometimes, in moments of great intensity, she would clench her hands and crouch. Seeing how the audience reacted to her, and how Noel and Peter were affirming her performance, she would respond with even greater intensity. Watching Mary perform was like watching a series of veils revealing ever-changing levels of great intimacy. Her performances declared her passions, her empathy, her determination, and her enormous love. It all came pouring out— love for the music, for the world, and of principle.

It is a remarkable experience for us to look at photos of the trio performing in the early years. For one thing, and this must be true for anyone looking at old photographs, we look so incredibly young. And Mary looks so startlingly beautiful. When you're together day in and day out, you tend to take this kind of thing for granted. Looking at the trio onstage at that time, there's a visual poetry in the folds of Mary's dress and the way her hair flows that is absolutely remarkable. They say that youth is wasted on the young and, in a similar sense, it's clear that what we were sharing was so natural, as well as all-consuming, that we really didn't have a sense of perspective about how unusual our lives were. In our later years together, particularly our last decade, we acquired a perspective that included a deep sense of appreciation for the privilege of what we shared as performers, friends, and activists. We lived our lives to the hilt in the early years and had the gift of greater appreciation as the years passed.

When the trio received a Grammy or some other award, Noel and Peter would haul out their "same old" black ties but, to our delight, Mary always surprised us with a new look that provided the luster for the occasion.

Lightning had struck. Almost every day, we were thrust into a new spotlight. During our first year of touring, we performed six concerts a week for almost twelve months straight. Among other remarkable adventures, we sang for President John F. Kennedy at the National Guard Armory in Washington, DC. At a party after the concert, we met the president in person. Amazing! The spotlight was thrown on us as we careened through a heady touring and concert schedule, a task that often required multiple connections on propeller-driven aircrafts. Our day-in, day-out, performances were predictably to full-house crowds of extremely generous college students who spoiled us with thunderous applause in campus auditoriums, gymnasiums, and field houses.

By our third year, several Bob Dylan songs graced our repertoire. The face of folk music was rapidly changing. Traditional songs were now accompanied by a fiercely powerful, new kind of lyric, sparked by a new vitality, immediacy, and a Dylanesque poetry that took us all by storm. Each night after the concerts, we'd sign autographs for a while and then sit down, sometimes for hours, with the late-staying students. Our conversations invariably centered around the enormous changes that were taking place in America as the Civil Rights Movement riveted the nation, the Women's Movement began to take shape, and the country began moving inexorably toward involvement in the Vietnam War and its fervent opposition.

We had an unspoken rule, intuitively agreed upon but never discussed: as much as possible, we wanted to imbue each song's performance with the spirit of first-night wonderment, discovery, and spontaneity. We tried to make each song's performance come alive with its own special chemistry as we searched for a song's relevance and meaning on that particular evening. We drew inspiration from the audiences and their responses, as well, which was an important part of the give and take of our shows. Our intuitive agreement to rediscover our songs anew each night meant that, on stage, we had to be intensely present and focused. For us, the stage was a kind of sacred place where we were committed to being the best that we could be. Offstage, like everyone, we had feet of clay: we were good and bad, faulted and sublime at times, just human beings.

Like Mary, Noel also had a dramatic presence onstage, both visually and physically. When he smiled, joked, or took on a new persona through his ingenious ability to bring imaginary people to life, his sweetness emerged, between and inside the laughter.

Peter was noted for his intensity and seriousness onstage, as well as his remarkable ability to get the audience to sing together passionately and beautifully, something he'd learned from Pete Seeger, the great master of sing-alongs.

Over the span of his forty years with the trio, travel with our bass player Dick Kniss (right) was always an adventure. Once, Dick made a domestic flight "substitution" where he departed on a flight to Greensboro, North Carolina, when he was actually ticketed on a flight to Greenville, South Carolina (honest . . . really happened). Equally at home on European jazz stages or in small folk clubs, Dick was a bassist who understood and responded authentically to the drama of the folk ballad. His underlining of each song's mood (from "Polly Von" to "Jet Plane") was a study in textures and sensitive counterpoint. Dick sometimes introduced the song with an arco figure (bowed bass), sometimes pizzicato, and sometimes he waited for the lyric to develop, his choice always better revealing the song's story.

The first time we met The Beatles was during our trip to London to sing for the Queen. We joined John, Paul, George, and Ringo on their film set for *A Hard Day's Night*, where we spent a few awkward moments vainly trying to find conversational connections. Finally, someone mercifully suggested that we all meet later at the Dorchester Hotel for a photo, a contrived opportunity that revealed more about a cultural impasse than a mutuality of music appreciation. We entered the room somewhat awkwardly and were asked to pose with The Beatles. Though everyone was polite, it was clear that no one felt really at ease. Ed Sullivan's surprise arrival provided a spontaneous burst of conversation, and two

Mary's style, onstage and off, was really a creative act. Buying "mod" boots in England, all the rage at the time, was a giggle, but not really characteristic of her taste. Mary's choices of clothes and costumes for the stage were similar to the choices she made when decorating, or finding works of art for, her home. A classical sense of style was hers from the time that she first had enough money to buy a couch, curtains, or simple gold bangles for her wrist—a new one each year for the first ten we were together.

photographers memorialized this unusual (for us) situation that had been arranged purely for commercial reasons.

As absurd as it now sounds, at the time, many people in the music industry were skeptical that The Beatles would succeed in America. Sid Bernstein, one of their promoters, privately said he was taking a "big chance" in bringing them over. Our manager, Albert Grossman, who was known far and wide for his ability to predict outcomes in the music world, literally bet Peter that The Beatles would flop in the US. Soon after, of course, The Beatles' popularity spoke for itself. Over time, our admiration and respect for the poetry in their music increased, and Noel introduced Beatles-like production style into our recordings, particularly on our 1968 album, *Late Again*.

Peter, Paul and Mary with The Beatles and Ed Sullivan

Our trip to England to sing for Queen Elizabeth in a command performance at Royal Albert Hall was filled with all of the excitement associated with London's rich history and new, stylish, "mod" charm. For Mary, there was a small anecdote that was set against the grandeur of the moment: "When we were presented to the Queen, I did the traditional curtsy. One of the boys accidentally stepped on the train of my dress, and when I attempted to stand up, I almost fell!"

Over the years, it sometimes rained when we performed outdoors—at the Carter Barron Amphitheatre in DC, at Chastain Park in Atlanta, at Red Rocks in Denver, and elsewhere. Seldom did we stop the concert and, in turn, our audience members would get out their ponchos and umbrellas and, with much-appreciated determination, stay too.

THE WHITE HOUSE
WASHINGTON

Dear Mr. Stookey:

I wish to thank you for your participation in the Second Inaugural Anniversary Salute.

It was a wonderful evening which was enjoyed by all.

Both Mrs. Kennedy and I are most grateful for your giving of your time and talent and for doing so much to make the evening a truly memorable one.

Sincerely,

Mr. Paul Stookey
c/o Peter, Paul and Mary
75 East 55th Street
New York City, New York

In early 1963, the trio performed in Washington to celebrate the second anniversary of John F. Kennedy's presidency. After the performance, Vice President Lyndon Johnson hosted a somewhat impromptu party at his home for the performers. The president requested that the artists sing a few more songs. First Lady Jackie Kennedy was present, too, and was delightful, warm, and friendly. The artists included Joan Sutherland, Carol Burnett, Yves Montand, Gene Kelly, and us, just to mention a few. After dinner, we started the performances with a rendition of "500 Miles" and a sing-along version of "Puff, the Magic Dragon." At one memorable point, the Persian carpet in the living room was rolled up for a rendition of "The Wearing of the Green" with the president singing along arm-in-arm with Gene Kelly, who did some incredible tap dance solos in the breaks.

After the performances, the president graciously came over to the performers to thank each of us, personally. When the president approached Noel, he asked, "What was the name of that song you sang when everyone applauded? They seemed to know the lyrics, as well."

"Oh," answered Peter, "that was 'If I Had a Hammer.' They knew the song because it was released as a single." Peter paused a moment, and then went on to explain, "A single is a recording of just one tune . . . put on a vinyl disc—"

"I know, I know," interrupted the president, smiling gently. "I just don't get much of a chance to listen to the radio while driving to work anymore."

Later that year, the trio was booked to do a performance in Dallas on November 23, the day after the president's arrival. As Noel remembers, "While driving from Houston, where we had performed the night before, Mary and I heard the news on the car radio. We were shocked, and mute. Like so many other Americans, our initial hopes were that the information was not true or that it had been exaggerated, or that even if such a thing were possible, of course the president would recover. If only one of those scenarios had been true . . . The president was officially pronounced dead by the time we arrived at our Dallas hotel. At 5 p.m., we joined Peter, who had arrived earlier. Within the hour Mary and I cancelled our concert and booked the next flight out of town. Peter rented a car and just drove and drove, leaving Dallas, until he hit another city from which he could fly back to New York."

IN PERSON
Sat. Nov. 23   8:30 PM
SMU COLISEUM
RESERVED SEATS $2.00 $1.00

TICKETS ON SALE AT:
STATE FAIR BOX OFFICE   TICKETS (WYNNEWOOD)
PRESTON STATE BANK   SHOEMAKER (RICHARDSON)
SMU STUDENT CENTER

In the early '60s, New York City coffeehouses were like classrooms. At the conclusion of an hour's presentation, both performer and audience would explore Bleecker or MacDougal Street for the next lesson. If these urban musical experiences were akin to attending Greenwich Village University, then the Newport Folk Festival was, by extension, summer school. For four days in July on the coast of Rhode Island, the space between artist and listener ceased to exist.

Although Newport's main stage performances were remarkable, many people experienced the essence of Newport in the smaller "workshops." In these gatherings, many of which spontaneously came together in a ballroom or on a lawn, musical styles and backgrounds intertwined—black, white, country, urban, youngsters, oldsters. People "jammed" together, picking, singing, and creating a universal language of music that was pure delight. The sounds of banjos, mandolins, fiddles, guitars, and voices filled the air. These workshop experiences reminded us that old barriers could, and were, coming down. They also revealed how meaningful and natural togetherness could be.

Newport became a beacon, a demonstration of our collective hopes and dreams for a better, more equitable, fairer world. The messages were personal, of course, but also, by implication, political. Newport was an example to the nation and the world of the loving power of music to build community, as Pete had taught us all.

Music and connections at the 1964 Newport Folk Festival, including Bob Dylan (top left); Mary and Len Chandler (middle); and Mary, Almeda Riddle, Robert Pete Williams, members of the Georgia Sea Island Singers, Reverend Robert Wilkins, and Joan Baez at an afternoon gospel music workshop (bottom, left to right)

P. O. Box 4761
Richmond, Virginia

Miss. Mary Travers
Messrs. Peter Yarrow and Paul Stookey
Warner Brothers Records, Inc.
666 Fifth Avenue
New York, New York

Dear Peter, Paul and Mary.

I would like to congratulate you on creating a beautiful sound. Your recordings are all done in the purest, plaintive simplicity. I enjoy listening to your records as much or more than those of any other current group.

However, the political ramifications of some of your songs should be pointed out to you. The lyrics of "Blowing in the Wind," for instance, contain several of the more obvious slogans of the Communists and Communists fronts. I wonder if the answer that's "blowing in the wind" is the hoped for (by some) take-over by Communism?

"Old Coat" sounds like a lament that some people are rich and others poor. The answer of course is Communism where everyone is equal-- equally poor. In this song it sounds as though the singer is sad because he is striving for social justice and society is persecuting him for his red views.

According to the <u>Daily Worker</u> the song "If I Had a Hammer" was first sung at a Communist rally in June 1949 to commemorate the trial of some Communist leaders. I understand Pete Seegar and Lee Hays hold the copyright on this song. Pete Seegar declined to tell the Congress whether or not he was a member of the Communist Party.

I was sorry to hear of your participation in the Washington Rally on August 28th. You probably did not know that the coordinator of the march was Bayard Rustin, former member of the Communist Party.

Sincerely yours,

E. G. Galleher

Left: Folk music and activism converge, blurring the lines between the stage and the world of struggle in the streets. The Freedom Singers, four black activists who had been on the marches and had received blows from policemen and Klansmen alike, joined our trio, Joan Baez, Bob Dylan, Pete Seeger, and Theo Bikel to sing "We Shall Overcome" at the Newport Folk Festival in 1963.

Billboard | For Week Ending December 14, 1963

TOP LP's

This Week	Last Week	Title, Artist, Label	Wks. on Chart
1	1	THE SINGING NUN .... Philips PCC 203 (M); PCC 603 (S)	6
2	2	IN THE WIND .... Peter, Paul & Mary, Warner Bros. W 1507 (M); WS 1507 (S)	8
3	3	THE SECOND BARBRA STREISAND ALBUM .... Columbia CL 2054 (M); CS 8854 (S)	14
4	5	TRINI LOPEZ AT PJ's .... Reprise R 6093 (M); R9-6093 (S)	22
5	6	ELVIS' GOLDEN RECORDS, VOL. 2 .... Elvis Presley, RCA Victor LPM 2765 (M); LSP 2765 (S)	14
6	10	INGREDIENTS IN A RECIPE FOR SOUL .... Ray Charles, ABC-Paramount ABC 465 (M); ABCS 465 (S)	16
7	4	PETER, PAUL & MARY .... Warner Bros. W 1449 (M); WS 1449 (S)	86
8	13	SURFER GIRL .... Beach Boys, Capitol T 1981 (M); ST 1981 (S)	10
9	7	WEST SIDE STORY .... Sound Track, Columbia OL 5670 (M); OS 2070 (S)	112
10	12	MOVING .... Peter, Paul & Mary, Warner Bros. W 1473 (M); WS 1473 (S)	48
11	15	WASHINGTON SQUARE .... Village Stompers, Epic LN 24078 (M); BN 26078 (S)	7
12	9	THE BARBRA STREISAND ALBUM .... Columbia CL 2007 (M); CS 8807 (S)	36
13	14	PAINTED, TAINTED ROSE .... Al Martino, Capitol T 1975 (M); ST 1975 (S)	10
14	11	THE JAMES BROWN SHOW	25

Peter, Paul and Mary's first single, "Lemon Tree," and our second, "If I Had a Hammer," both from our first album, sped up the charts, remaining in the Top Ten for many, many months. Although we were delighted with this achievement, we were so absorbed in the joy and wonderment of performing together, that, to a large degree, we were oblivious to how unusual such high-velocity success was in the record industry.

The trio performs in a television appearance with Andy Williams (far right) in 1966.

In the months and years that followed, we often participated in social/political movement marches and demonstrations. We knew that our involvement in some events could cost us fans and sales. When Mary and Harry Belafonte hugged and kissed each other in celebration after we sang together on the steps of the Montgomery State Capitol building, the final destination of the Selma–Montgomery march of 1965, it was viewed as heresy in some parts of America—a grave insult to those who still carried the cruel banner of segregation. Our record label, Warner Bros. Records, predicted that if we participated in the Selma–Montgomery Civil Rights March, we would lose much of our Southern market, which was a significant part of our record-buying audience. Warner Bros. was right about the loss of sales but, to their credit, they never discouraged us from participating in such appearances that were, after all, at the heart of what bound us together.

Compared to the courage of the civil rights workers who faced daily beatings, jail, and death, the danger to us, and what we sacrificed, was minimal. Those who marched and put their lives on the line paid the price and lit the way. They lived their lives with extreme courage, enduring punishment, suffering, and great loss, but, at great cost to themselves, pursued change with a peaceful and loving spirit. They were beyond heroes to us. Pete Seeger, The Weavers, and others who had traveled this folk singers' road before us also lit the way. We, in turn, followed their lead in a shared commitment to try and make our nation more just.

Above: The trio joins Dr. Martin Luther King Jr., who led the bloody and historic Civil Rights March from Selma, Alabama, to the state capitol in Montgomery.

Left: This aerial view shows a half-mile-long column of civil rights demonstrators, led by Dr. Martin Luther King Jr., on March 21, 1965, in Selma, Alabama, on the last leg of the Selma–Montgomery March as the demonstrators crossed the Edmund Pettus Bridge. The bridge was the scene of a violent attack by state troopers, now called Bloody Sunday, which took place two weeks earlier, the first time the marchers tried to cross it.

Years later, Mary reflected in a column in the *Bucks County Courier Times:* "During the Civil Rights Marches in the '60s, I often marched side by side with my mother. She told me of the great labor demonstrations of the '30s, and encouraged me in the belief that peaceful protest was an honorable tradition. She taught me to value accountability, responsibility, and continuity. So as I stood in the cold, wet Washington morning at yet another protest march, with my arm around my daughter, I told her about Daniel Ellsberg. That's what moms are for."

Echo of Alabama March

Odor 'Bomb' Fails to Halt Peter, Paul, Mary Singing

The stench at the Peter, Paul and Mary show at the Tulsa Civic Assembly Center Friday night came not from the performance, but apparently from someone who thought the singers should have stayed in Alabama. Before a stench "bomb" caused a stir among an estimated audience of 6,000, a lone picket had walked outside the building carrying a sign advising the singing team to "Go Back to Selma."

The entertainers had performed at Montgomery for civil rights marchers who made the trek from Selma to the state capital.

There was no wholesale exit from the arena when the fumes became evident, Dan Saunders, assistant manager of the building, said. He said perhaps several hundred people stirred around, but returned to their seats shortly for the remainder of the show.

THE STENCH WAS FIRST noticed about a half hour after the show got under way at 9:05 p.m., 35 minutes later than scheduled, because of plane trouble the singers had run into in Texas earlier in the day.

Saunders said an off-duty policeman found a four-ounce bluing bottle, with a rag stuck in the neck, on the east side of the arena among the permanent seats near the top.

Only about an ounce of the stench fluid remained in the bottle, the rest apparently having soaked into the rag "wick."

Saunders said when the odor was first noticed, the fire department and gas company were called. He said it was quickly determined that there was no gas leak.

A MEETING OF U.S. JUNIOR Chamber of Commerce directors in one of the rooms at the center also was disrupted for a while.

To help speed the removal of the "rotten egg" odor in the auditorium, a chemical deodorizer was introduced into the fresh air ducts.

The singers, Mary Allin Travers, Peter Yarrow and Paul Stookey continued to perform during the disturbance.

Earlier, the audience had become anxious about their late appearance on stage and had begun to clap. Three minutes late the trio appeared on stage and greeted their audience with a favorite number, "Lemon Tree," followed by "That's What You Get For Lovin' Me."

After this Paul did his own rendition of "Goldfinger" only to find during the middle of the act that his audience in the upper regions of the Civic Center were rapidly diminishing.

PAUL MADE A FEW "cracks" about the situation then the three carried out the age-old tradition of 'the show must go on'.

Certainly, some people sent us clear messages, both verbally and nonverbally, to just "shut up and sing." Beyond losing a portion of our audience, we often had to decide whether to perform in circumstances where there were announced threats. We never really took such threats seriously (or at least never admitted to it), though in the back of our minds we knew well that many had died in the struggle for peace and justice. For instance, we were told that we would be killed if we went on the Civil Rights March in Frankfort, Kentucky. At the time, Mary was pregnant with her second daughter, Alicia, and the issue felt graver than usual. Fortunately, the only bomb at the concert ended up being a smoke bomb.

One tragically memorable occasion that brought the sacrifice of others into focus in a deeply painful way was our singing "Blowin' in the Wind" at the graveside installation of Andrew Goodman's headstone. Andrew, along with his friends, James Chaney and Michael Schwerner, were the students murdered by Ku Klux Klansmen when they went to Mississippi to register African-American voters in April of 1964. Carolyn Goodman, Andy's mother and an indomitable organizer, had asked us to share this moment with her and the family. She made it clear that our singing for Andy meant the world to her. Of course, this moment remained an unforgettable memory for the trio.

The Selma–Montgomery March focused on people of color's right to vote, and was one of the great political and emotional peaks of the 1960s' Civil Rights Movement. On March 7, 1965, known as Bloody Sunday, more than six hundred civil rights marchers were attacked by state and local police. The trio, and others who had played the night before in a muddy field in St. Jude, had been transported to Montgomery, so we were not part of that brutal confrontation.

OFFICE OF

COMMISSIONER OF THE REVENUE

ROANOKE COUNTY · TOWN OF SALEM

J. LUCK RICHARDSON, JR., COMMISSIONER

SALEM, VIRGINIA

Mr. Stephen A. Anderson
2523 Rosalind Ave.
Roanoke, Virginia

Peter, Paul, and Mary:

My neighbor and Myself have been admirers of your
talent for sometime now and have purchased nearly all
of your albums and singles to date.
So, by our being born Southerners here in Virginia,
we were greatly conserned with your supporting the
peaceful negro demenstrations in Washington a short time
ago.
For my own personal reasons I would like to know,
and therefor understand, your motivation for joining
the Marchers. Could it have been for publisity or
recognition, were you paid for your services, or would
it be that you believe strongly in the American Negro
Cause?
You and I are both quite aware that your main
support comes from White people and so I being one of
your many admirers believe you owe me an explanation
of these happenings.
I agree that any body of peaceful citizens has the
right to assemble in our country, but the motivation
was FEAR and was COMMUNISTIC supported, planned, and
inspired.
It is an old story, the negro has the Mark of Cain
and has for centuries been a beast of burden, no man
in this country or any other is created equal. You make
of yourself what you have the mind and initiative to
aquire, white or black it makes no difference.
I don't hate anyone, but I have a daughter a year
and a half old and I don't want her to go to school, eat
with, or mix with any negro. As Lincoln himself said:
there is a dividing line, a limit that each side should
abide by.
Come to Roanoke or a hundred-thousand other Southern
towns and cities and see if you could possibly conceive
of sending a child of yours to school with the class of
Negro we have here. Of hiring them on the bacis that
they wish to aquire, living beside them. In general
watching your children, school systems, and businesses,
being brought down to a very low level.

Right: The trio performs for a large crowd at the Bryant Park War Moratorium in New York City. By late 1969, when this photograph was taken, singing songs at demonstrations to rally the spirit of the crowd, and speaking out from our collective point of view, had become as much a way of life as doing concerts. There was a euphoria that came with these performances: when you stand in front of a large group of people all singing together, you feel the strength of their dedication to a cause, and you fully believe that things will change for the better. Sometimes, as with the great marches in which the trio participated, it seemed as if there was no way to stop the tide of caring and unanimity of spirit we were sharing. In fact, it often felt as if the objective of the march or demonstration had, if only for a moment, actually been achieved. As time passed, we learned that these moments of intense hope were only stepping stones—powerful stepping stones, to be sure—but only some of the steps in a long march that would take enormous effort and dedication and many years to claim even partial victory.

From backstage at coffeehouses to bowties at the Grammys, the intimacy and directness of American folk music was quickly transcending cultural norms. By the mid '60s, fans in France, Germany, and Japan were singing songs such as "500 Miles" and "If I Had a Hammer." The popular rise of the idiom was so baffling to the recording industry and the average music listener that the once predictable methods of measuring success in the music business failed. *Billboard* and *Cashbox*, two venerable weeklies of the times, did their best to assess this musical bubble by simply reporting record sales, but they were unable to find a name for the folk phenomenon. Strangely, even jazz polls began to feature folk performers among their ranks of top artists.

Above: Mary holds the trio's Grammy at the 12th Annual Grammy Awards. Merv Griffin and Brenda Lee are seated next to her. In the years when we released our first three albums, the frequency with which the trio received acknowledgments and awards was dizzying. At first the captains of the music business were mystified by the unexpected surge in folk music's popularity, but they were nevertheless gracious and welcomed us as the (somewhat odd) newbies into their family.

Left: Noel and Richie Havens backstage during the 11th Annual Grammy Awards. Richie was, in many ways, the trio's favorite singer. On and offstage, he walked the walk of a person filled with grace, and dedicated to a higher purpose. A more loving and caring human being one could not find, and his friendship with the trio was a precious gift. Richie is truly missed.

Left: In Paris, we performed at the Olympia, the famous small theater that previously hosted the royalty of French singers such as Yves Montand, Edith Piaf, and the like. Peter knew French, so he introduced all the songs—and when he sang *"Le Déserteur,"* an anti-war song that, at the time, was forbidden on the radio, the audience responded with an explosion of applause.

HOLIDAY IN JAPAN

In the mid and late '60s, the trio ventured outside the United States. The welcome we received from the Japanese people was remarkable. Though they were shy to sing along or applaud energetically, their appreciation was palpable—and so it was that some of the most passionate performances of our career were delivered in Tokyo, Osaka, and Kyoto.

The Vietnam Anti-War Movement emerged right out of the Civil Rights Movement. In fact, it stood on the shoulders of the solidarity that had been created when our country finally stood up for justice on behalf of people of color. Our country had started to pave the way for what has now been almost fifty years of eradicating much, but certainly not all, of the remnants of our wretched and shameful history of slavery. As a consequence of the Civil Rights Movement, there emerged in America a hunger to be proud of who we were and to insist that we not just give lip service to being a moral nation. Our young soldiers had started coming home in body bags from an (undeclared) war in Vietnam that, to us, was based on a deliberate stream of lies from the Pentagon that falsely justified our continuing pursuit of the war. Never, to us, was it credible to assert that, in fighting Vietnam, our country was protecting itself from foreign aggression. Further, the draft was compelling young men to participate in the war or go to jail unless they had been granted conscientious objector status. Now the same youths who had turned this nation around in the Civil Rights Movement began mobilizing to protest the war, and our nation started to painfully split along a line of demarcation—hawks and doves, progressives and conservatives—that still exists today. Civil discourse and middle ground had begun to erode.

Peter, Paul and Mary continued pursuing our activist efforts. In many ways, activism had become as

Peter, Paul and Mary perform to 200,000 demonstrators at a 1969 major anti-war demonstration in front of the UN Building in New York City.

much our central identity as our being makers of music. Folk music, and its inclusive message, allowed us to make an appeal to a very broad spectrum of people across partisan and ideological divides. Our concerts always contained songs such as "Where Have All the Flowers Gone," "Blowin' in the Wind," "When the Ship Comes In," "The Times They Are a-Changin'," "If I Had a Hammer," and "The Great Mandala," a powerful anti-war song written by Peter. However, in addition to singing our songs with their frequently pointed content, we wanted our views on the war to be expressed, verbally, as often as possible: in our concerts, in radio and TV interviews, and at demonstrations and marches specifically focused on rallying support for ending the war.

We never liked it when people labeled our music as "protest songs." For us, the songs were affirmations that invariably pointed to a path that, we felt, could resolve problems through peaceful means. One of the virtues of folk songs is that their lyrics and their message are far less likely to be dismissed as polemic than if the same lyrics were simply spoken. Through our mentors, we had learned that songs could bypass long-held barriers and go right to the heart of listeners, so we were grateful to find that "fence-sitters"—and even people who disagreed with our politics—came to our concerts and embraced our music. Singing and speaking to these mixed audiences was important. We came to realize that our songs might well move some members of the crowd who disagreed with us to consider our point of view.

The oppositional split in America deepened as the war progressed, with increasing anger between the two sides as the tragedy of the war intensified. War supporters felt that those who opposed it were unpatriotic, cowardly, anti-American, or worse—"Pinkos" or "Commie sympathizers" whose activist efforts were tantamount to sedition. Those of us who opposed the war viewed its continuation as immoral, based upon mistaken thinking or outright lies, which made us angry, ashamed, and far less naïve about the political realities of our times.

Our young men continued to die, uselessly in our view, as did the Vietnamese people. By the end of the war, we had killed some three million people—soldiers and noncombatants. The United States had lost more than 58,000 soldiers. Thousands more soldiers came home to suffer greatly with terrible wounds and post-traumatic stress disorder symptoms. Perhaps worse, returning vets were treated as a disgrace by anti-war protesters.

Mary speaks at an anti–Vietnam War leaders' news conference in New York in 1967.

Quirky in the extreme, perhaps, but it was still quite a compliment for Peter, Paul and Mary to be included in this *Mad* magazine cartoon drawing along with The Beatles, Louis Armstrong, Barbra Streisand, Soviet leader Nikita Khrushchev, Mao Tse-tung, Alfred E. Neuman, the Brooklyn Dodgers, the New York Yankees, and the New York Giants.

Added to the suffering they endured in the war, this reception was humiliating and gravely damaging to them, and one more reason that many returned soldiers' personal lives were all but impossible to put back together. Many were lost to suicide and drug addiction after their return. In fact, as many were lost in these ways as were lost in the war itself. How cruel and unfair it was for any of us who protested the war to blame the warrior, rather than, simply and understandably, to abominate the war. It was tragic, utterly tragic, and as the Civil Rights Movement shaped the trio, the war in Vietnam sharpened our perspective as activists and advocates with a new, and frequently painful, awareness.

Like others in the Anti-War Movement, sometimes we became verbal targets of war supporters. The issues were too volatile and too sensitive not to ignite passions on both sides. This was particularly true in the case of soldiers who had died or who had come home horribly wounded. The despair and anger of these military families was completely understandable, and it was undoubtedly painful for people to imply that their son, friend, or relative had died for a lie.

In the late '60s, the trio made a trip to Walter Reed National Military Medical Center, where we sang for Vietnam veterans. It was heartbreaking, and clear to us that these men, wounded in body and spirit, were among the most damaged victims of the war. They asked for us to sing "Leaving on a Jet Plane," of course, but also "Where Have All the Flowers Gone." Some thanked us for our opposition to the war, as did hundreds of Vietnam vets who approached us at concerts in later years, often tearfully.

On a sunny afternoon in May of 1970, we arrived by helicopter at the Illinois State Penitentiary in Joliet. We had been invited to perform by the Department of Corrections, and more than 2,200 inmates were waiting for us, sitting in anticipation on the prison's bleachers. As James Farnham reported in the prison's monthly newsletter (aptly named *TIME),* "The men were somewhat skeptical of the announcement that *the* Peter, Paul and Mary were coming to entertain. When the celebrated folk singing trio stepped to the microphones and virtually shattered the gloom of Stateville with their golden voices, their doubt ended. They were here! In person!!"

We opened with "The Hour the Ship Comes In" and then moved to "Leaving on a Jet Plane," the trio's recent hit on the charts. Mary was definitely the inmates' focus for the first few songs. Our socially conscious lyrics had less impact on the inmates than the physical energy Mary brought to the stage. The applause and cheering began almost immediately, continued through the entire first song, and went on for a full minute after we finished, creating its own sound as their claps echoed off the building's brick walls. Mary seemed a little embarrassed by the prisoners' roaring response to what was, after all, her natural performance style.

We sang not only to entertain, but also to soothe and reassure, and soon the inmates seemed to connect deeply with our songs of alienation and loneliness. Peter invited the prisoners to sing along with "Oh, Rock My Soul," dividing them into three groups, each with their own part. On that sunny day in a penitentiary, thousands of voices sang:

Rock my soul in the bosom of Abraham.
Rock my soul in the bosom of Abraham.
Rock my soul in the bosom of Abraham. Oh, rock my soul.

So high I can't get over it.
So low I can't get under it.
So wide I can't get round it.
Oh, rock my soul.

We praised the staff and administration for their reform efforts and dedicated "The Times They Are a-Changin'" to them, and then closed the show with "If I Had a Hammer." After a standing ovation that lasted a really long time, we left in the same helicopter in which we arrived. The prison's newsletter quoted one of the long-term inmates as saying, "If someone had told me a couple of years ago that Peter, Paul and Mary would be coming here to entertain the cons, I probably would have said, 'Sure, and the warden is going to give all of us machine guns, too.'"

The trio performs outdoors at the Illinois State Penitentiary near Joliet, Illinois, 1970.

Above: Peter talks with civil rights activist, politician, and writer Julian Bond.
Top right: Mary talks with the iconic actor/singer and civil rights organizer Harry Belafonte backstage at the Winter Concert for Peace held at Madison Square Garden in 1970.

In the 1960s, Cesar Chavez, like Martin Luther King Jr. before him, became the central leader in the struggle of migrant workers for livable working conditions and pay that allowed more than bare subsistence. Cesar and his co-leader of the United Farm Workers (UFW), Dolores Huerta, organized a national boycott of grapes, one of the most profitable crops in America. Grapes were harvested through backbreaking work, mostly by Mexican migrant workers. Their suffering was, like that of America's people of color—who were prevented from voting, segregated, denied upward mobility, lynched without legal repercussion, and more—a source of national shame. Mega-farm corporations tried to defeat the boycott in a campaign with enormous funding that, consequently, gave them huge political clout. A vicious battle between corporate interests and the terribly exploited workers ensued.

Chavez used nonviolent means to achieve his objectives and went on highly visible, sometimes life-threatening, fasts, sometimes for weeks at a time, which, very effectively, spread awareness of the boycott and mobilized support. Ultimately the boycott shifted public opinion and the Grape Pickers' Strike succeeded in breaking generations of worker abuse. Robert Kennedy, attorney general in his brother's, President John F. Kennedy's, administration, became a huge champion of the UFW's cause. The trio was sympathetic to the grape pickers' boycott and participated along with millions of other Americans. Therefore, when we were asked to perform as part of a Carnegie Hall benefit concert to support the UFW, we were honored to accept the invitation.

Milton Glaser, the internationally acclaimed graphic designer who led Push Pin Studios and created all of the graphics for our record albums, stationery, and many other projects, asked his colleague, Paul Davis, who later became an iconic graphic designer/painter in his own right, to create the now-famous image of a young Hispanic boy that was featured in the poster for this concert. Over the years, Milt, Paul, Seymour Chwast, and George Leavitt from Push Pin were always willing to donate their artistic talents to advocacies that Peter, Paul and Mary embraced. Designers, singers, painters, songwriters, theater folk, and dance companies who championed the movements of the '60s all played a significant role in expressing the vision, carrying the message, and advancing the progress of social and political change.

We didn't plan to stop performing. We needed to, and, on a gut level, it just seemed like the right thing to do. We had traveled almost incessantly for ten years, and our 1969 schedule had been packed with more than two hundred concerts in five countries, as well as the recording and promoting of two new albums. Peter, Paul and Mary had become a compacted bundle of overwhelming commitments that did not allow enough time and space to accommodate our work as members of the trio and as individual artists who also needed to enjoy the rewards of family life.

When the tour concluded in Japan at the end of the year, it marked the beginning of what we referred to later—in far less serious terms than we did in 1970—as "seven years off for good behavior." Of course, there were other factors that contributed to the sudden cessation of our touring and recording. In large part, though, and in very different and personal ways, we came to see our time apart as being a blessing and a gift to all of us.

In 1972, we received a surprise phone call from Warren Beatty on behalf of George McGovern's presidential campaign with an invitation for us to perform at a fund-raising concert called "Together for McGovern" to be held at Madison Square Garden in New York City. "Dionne Warwick is coming out of retirement," he said. "We're bringing Simon and Garfunkel back and reuniting Mike Nichols and Elaine May. If you say yes, we'll also have Peter, Paul and Mary!"

Above: Senator George McGovern greets Mary at a 1972 rally in his support at New York's Madison Square Garden. Also included are Art Garfunkel (far left), Peter, Paul Simon, and McGovern's wife, Eleanor.

Warren's enthusiasm was infectious, and we accepted his invitation. Although none of us expressed expectations of concerts beyond appearing together for McGovern, joining our trio once more for something bigger than ourselves had a familiar, prophetic quality. The seeds of reunion had been sown.

The afternoon of the event brought everyone together for a sound check, including the senator. Warren had arranged for a brigade of Hollywood ushers, among them

Above: Peter at the mic **Top left:** Jack Nicholson and Warren Beatty during Madison Square Garden sound check **Top right:** Noel talks with Paul Simon and Art Garfunkel.

Goldie Hawn, Paul Newman, Lee Grant, Dustin Hoffman, and Jack Nicholson, to assist with the event, which added to a dazzling backstage chaos.

A modest Midwesterner, Senator McGovern seemed stunned by the celebrity factor, and he quickly sought out Mary for a comforting welcome.

Above: Peter and Mary talk with James Taylor and John Hall of Orleans. Hall was a central organizer of the Anti-Nuke Movement and, later, a member of Congress.

Left: The trio performs at the 1978 Hollywood Bowl concert, which was organized to prevent a proposed nuclear plant at Diablo Canyon, situated not far from an earthquake fault, from going online.

Opposite page, top: Senator Eugene McCarthy, statesman, poet, scholar, and Peter, Paul and Mary's revered hero whom they supported in his almost-successful primary presidential campaign in 1968, delivers an address to the 1978 Survival Sunday attendees.

During the trio's time apart, Peter continued to organize movement events, and in 1978 he co-organized an anti-nuclear gathering called Survival Sunday at the Hollywood Bowl. This event was part of the first international environmental movement that focused on stopping nuclear power plants ("nukes") from going online. It successfully halted the building of some new nukes, and worked to shut down nukes that were considered unsafe. Though the accidents at Three Mile Island, Chernobyl, and Fukushima had yet to occur, those attending Survival Sunday rightly considered these plants to be gravely dangerous. As with the demonstrations in the Anti-War Movement, performers and public spokespersons were called upon to stir the crowd to action. In the case of Survival Sunday, the objective was to prevent Diablo Canyon, a new Northern California plant that had been built right next to the San Andreas earthquake fault, from going online. Longtime allies from earlier social/political struggles were approached by Peter to join the demonstration, including Senator Gene McCarthy, Cesar Chavez, Mike Farrell, Allard Lowenstein, Robin Williams, Tom Paxton, Sweet Honey in the Rock, and George Carlin. Peter notes, "As in years past, I called upon my allies and singing partners, Mary and Noel, and asked them to participate. Though the trio had not sung together since the McGovern event, six years earlier, I had faith that they would want to be part of such an important demonstration supporting such an urgent cause. To my great personal delight, and relief as an organizer, they both eagerly agreed." Hearing us sing together again after such a long hiatus, the crowd greeted us like long-lost friends, cheering us and making us feel accepted and valued in this moment of reunification. Activism and advocacy were in our blood and the call to action was all but irresistible. We were back. And not just to sing, but singing for a cause—our

heart's home and, in many ways, our most comfortable turf. As Mary later said, "We wanted to work together enough to have it be a meaningful part of our lives, but not so much that it wouldn't be fun. We realized that we'd missed each other personally and musically, so we decided to try a limited reunion."

Our new performance schedule was about sixty shows a year. Compared to our early years, when we performed up to two hundred concerts a year, the new schedule was much reduced, allowing us to concertize and make records, while also pursuing personal projects and spending essential and much-needed time with our friends and families.

Twenty-fifth anniversaries are rare for musical groups, so, when our trio reached age twenty-five, we decided we would celebrate the year in several special ways, reflecting both our musical journey and our commitment as advocates. First, we returned to The Bitter End, the Village coffeehouse where we had performed our first "gig." About 250 people jammed into that now-iconic space where we, Bob Dylan, Joni Mitchell, and numerous other folk hopefuls had begun our careers. Proceeds from the ticket sales were donated to the Charity Bailey Fund, recognizing the amazingly gifted singer and world-renowned teacher who brought roots music to many of America's children and, coincidentally, to the Little Red School House that Mary attended as a child. At the end of the show, some of our dearest performing friends—Judy Collins, Paul Butterfield, John Denver, and Richie Havens—joined us onstage for our final songs.

Above: The trio celebrates with John Denver. **Top right:** Mary and Richie Havens **Right:** Mary and Theo Bikel

The trio performing at the twenty-fifth anniversary of the March on Washington in 1988

From left to right: Ken Fritz, Peter, friend, Judy Collins, Howard Metzenbaum, Odetta, Mary, and Harry Belafonte

The next celebration of our twenty-fifth year was the brainchild of Kenny Fritz, our manager at the time, who broke with Albert Grossman's view that television overexposed artists, watering down their artistry and presenting them in ways that, to Albert, felt synthetic and, in some ways, disrespectful. Kenny, however, quite rightly understood that in this later era, such protection from the media was no longer needed, at least in one particular context—PBS. Kenny felt that Peter, Paul and Mary's TV home needed to be PBS because of its natural alliance of viewer-sponsored programming and folk music, rather than our appearing on "commercial" TV, which tended to regard folk songs as oddities, "novelty tunes" of a sort. PBS, on the other hand, was more committed to substance than to chasing new and fleeting popular styles, and in our trio, the network found a willing ally in its goals. We embraced the PBS network's national obligation and charge: to present programming that served the public, programming that was provocative, informative, and inspiring. Commercial TV was, on the other hand, designed mostly to satisfy the monetary objectives of advertisers who wanted to sell their products. Quite a difference.

Starting with our twenty-fifth anniversary pledge special, and during the following two decades, the trio taped five 90-minute PBS specials. Ultimately, we were seen by more viewers during each PBS pledge period than ever saw us live, in concert, over our entire career.

Kenny also conceived of a special two-week run of Peter, Paul and Mary concerts on Broadway at the renowned Minskoff Theatre that he named "From Bleecker to Broadway." To create the graphics and stage design for that concert, we once again reached out to the designer of our album covers, Milton Glaser and his team. Among the graphic pieces created for this event was a huge, beautiful poster that was sniped—that is, literally pasted up on buildings and fences, mostly illegally—all over the city. The excitement and buzz of this campaign was a true first for us as we had never been treated to such a dazzling public relations outreach.

It seemed only appropriate to unite this anniversary with our twenty-five years of activism by creating a special project relating to one of the most painful

Above (left to right): Richie Havens, Mary, John Denver, Judy Collins, Noel, Peter, and Paul Butterfield
Top right: Albert Grossman and Peter's mother, Vera Yarrow   **Right:** The trio at The Bitter End, reprising the photograph on their first album cover taken twenty-five years earlier

problems facing New York: homelessness and the apparent lack of understanding about who the homeless population really was and how people became drawn into this painful reality. We learned a great deal about homelessness in a meeting with Bob Hayes, a McCarthy Genius Award recipient who had left a lucrative legal career at a top corporate law firm, Sullivan & Cromwell, to create the Coalition for the Homeless. Bob was greatly admired for his efforts to correct the public's misperceptions of homelessness's root causes, and for his tireless advocacies to change the laws governing the treatment of the homeless. We also met with Michael Posner, who led the Lawyers Committee for Human Rights, a group that had an international reach, but Michael also knew the nonprofit landscape of New York City

inside and out. Michael and Bob helped to arrange a series of visits by the trio to homeless shelters: one a women-only shelter, another for women with children, and another for men only.

We were shocked to learn that the majority of the homeless population consisted of children living with single mothers who were forced onto the streets because of job loss, mental or physical illness, or domestic violence. On these visits we were accompanied on one occasion by the iconic leader of the UFW (United Farm Workers), Cesar Chavez; on another occasion by Ruth Messinger, a great humanitarian activist and a member of the New York City Council at the time; and on a third visit by David Dinkins, the Manhattan borough president who would later become mayor of NYC. During each visit we sang and afterward spent time listening to what were frequently heartbreaking, but also inspiring, stories of courage and resilience shared by the residents and staff of the shelters.

After educating ourselves through this direct exposure to the homeless population, we went on a tour of radio stations in New York City and shared what we had learned about the true nature of homelessness in on-air interviews. Our intent was to add our voices to the efforts of many others who sought to help correct the public's misconceptions about homelessness, to help reframe the

Above left (top and bottom) and opposite page middle and far right: The trio listens to the moving stories of homeless shelter residents. **Above right:** Cesar Chavez (far left) joins the trio in conversations with homeless shelter residents.

dialogue and policies regarding the homeless population, and to lobby for increased funding to ease the suffering of this much-maligned and misunderstood population.

In the Minskoff Theatre's lobby, we mounted an exhibition by Marilynne Herbert, the gifted photographer of our visits to the shelters. We also donated the concert's opening-night proceeds to the Coalition for the Homeless and organized an after-concert high-donor gathering at Nathan's Famous hot dog establishment on Broadway. These special events, taken together, gave us a wonderful and fitting way to celebrate our twenty-fifth.

In June of 1983, we were invited to perform in Israel at a very famous and ancient outdoor venue in Jerusalem called Sultan's Pool. More than ten thousand people attended, and the group honored the miracle of Israel's having transformed the desert into a vibrant and remarkable country that had come so far in such a short period of time. We sang the first touring concert performance of "Light One Candle," the Chanukah song that Noel and Mary had asked Peter to write for the trio's Carnegie Hall holiday concerts.

This was our first trip to Israel, and on the first day we toured Yad Vashem, a painfully revealing museum memorializing the Jewish victims of the Holocaust. The museum also honored the many people who, frequently in peril of their lives, had sheltered or sought to save victims of the Nazi genocide. It was a wrenching experience, to say the least, and we came away deeply moved and shaken.

The relationship between Israel and Palestine, at the time, was not what it became in the mid-1980s, when the First Intifada captured the world stage, highlighting an increasingly dangerous and painful situation. Our first trip was devoid of political examinations and heartrending dialogues that would later modify, and cast a cloud over, our first idyllic impressions.

The trio plants a tree in Israel to honor the Israeli tradition of planting trees to mark births, deaths, and religious milestones.

In 1986, the trio traveled to El Salvador and Nicaragua. We were not newcomers to the challenges that plagued these countries. Mary had made previous trips to El Salvador where, traumatically, she encountered the bodies of people killed by an explosion on a bus traveling ahead of her. Noel had written what became one of the trio's most compelling and heartbreaking songs, "El Salvador," which condemned the policies of our own country that supported and financed President Duarte's cruelly oppressive regime.

From Noel's diary during the trio's El Salvador trip:

The press conference at the conclusion of the trio's El Salvador/Nicaragua trip takes place in a meeting room at our Managua hotel. The three of us, our translator, and Janet Shenk, a wonderful political organizer who was leading our trip, leads us to a table and cluster of eight or nine microphones. In attendance are stringers for the networks and Television Nicaragua. To begin, Peter welcomes everyone and speaks of our purpose in visiting Central America. "We came to learn about the situation so that we might better understand what is clearly a very complex issue," he says. The first reporter asks, "What have you seen here?" Mary answers, broadly, informatively, telling of the people we met and, at the end, commenting on "our ever-present awareness that there is a war going on here."

A reporter standing in the back asks how we feel about the Contra-aid bill being recently passed by Congress. I begin to answer but break down after a sentence or two. Peter and Mary reach to take my hand, and then to touch my arm. "So when you ask what we feel about the approval of Contra-aid . . . what I remember most . . ." I hesitated, ". . . is a priest holding this white flower above his head and saying, 'This is a flower of peace . . . take it to the American people and ask them please not to pour our blood on it.'" There are tears running down my cheeks and there is a hush. Peter attempts to answer the next question but now, for each of us, there comes a moment of overwhelming personal recall and the breakdown happens again . . . Mary confesses that

Mary listens to the stories and travail of El Salvadorians on her first trip to Central America, two years before the trio's journey there.

we've been doing press conferences for twenty-five years in countries all over the world and that this is the first time we have ever been so emotional. A few minutes later, the conference is over and we stand next to the table with our arms around each other . . . this has been the most galvanizing experience of our PP&M lives.

Later in the same year, Mary discussed her Central America activism work in an interview with the *Bucks County Courier Times*:

I have no vested interest in preserving the Sandinista government; that is for the Nicaraguan people to decide. But I do have a vested interest in preserving my country's commitment to democracy and its political traditions. To do that you have to ask questions. I have, and I didn't like all the answers.

The trio joins South African Bishop Desmond Tutu (front left) at an anti-apartheid rally with TransAfrica leader Randall Robinson (back left).

Desmond Tutu and Noel

In January of 1986, we participated in a rally in Washington, DC, that supported the US boycott of South Africa. The boycott had, amazingly, become US law through an override of President Reagan's veto, and had become a means to successfully pressure the South African government to end apartheid's near-slavery conditions. Bishop Desmond Tutu spoke at that rally in his first US appearance since winning the 1984 Nobel Peace Prize. We sang "No Easy Walk to Freedom," written by Peter for the occasion that linked Martin Luther King and Nelson Mandela, who became the first post-apartheid president of South Africa subsequent to his release after twenty-seven years in jail.

The day after this rally, in a planned act of civil disobedience, we convened on the South African embassy's front steps. We locked arms and began singing "We Shall Overcome," deliberately standing in what was supposed to be a protest-free zone. Our group included the trio; Mary's mother and one of her daughters, Alicia; Peter's daughter, Bethany; and two rabbis, including David Saperstein, the famous head of the Union of American Hebrew Congregations' Religious Action Center (RAC) where the Civil Rights Acts had been signed. The police arrived and told us to disperse, but we continued to sing. After more warnings, we were handcuffed, arrested, and taken to DC Jail. The jail had already received our Social Security numbers, as it had been pre-informed of our intentions. Mary sometimes recalled the event onstage, triumphantly noting, "It was great—three generations in handcuffs." Actually, the trio's arrest was preceded by the arrests of more than twelve hundred US citizens and about the same number thereafter, including many members of Congress. All these acts of civil disobedience helped to keep the Anti-Apartheid Boycott on the front pages, strengthening what ultimately became a clear victory of grassroots activism.

Peter, Paul and Mary with friends and family sing in a "no-protest zone" in front of the South African Embassy in Washington, DC, prior to being arrested for civil disobedience. This was part of a similar action taken by almost three thousand others who were arrested over a two-year period, including many members of Congress, all of whom were supporting the US trade and divestment boycott of South Africa that helped to end the cruel apartheid system. This action also lent support to black South Africans' demand for the release of Nelson Mandela after twenty-seven years in jail. From left to right are Noel; Peter; Mary; Mary's daughter, Alicia; Ken Fritz, the trio's manager (behind Alicia); and Mary's mother, Virginia.

Above (from left to right): Shelley Belusar, Peter, Dave Tkachuk, Peter's daughter Bethany, Dick Kniss, Mary, and Noel backstage **Top left:** Peter and sound designer and live sound mixer Dave Tkachuk **Middle left:** Trio rehearsing with music director Bob DeCormier **Bottom left:** Shelley Belusar (left), the trio's beloved tour manager and lighting designer for thirty years, at the light board, and the always-colorful Paul Prestopino (right)

In 2003, the trio released *Carry It On,* a boxed set of four CDs spanning our career to that point. A DVD included in the package showed footage of "If I Had a Hammer" at the 1963 Civil Rights March on Washington. Coretta Scott King, Dr. King's widow and a great activist in her own right, wrote a tribute, quoted in the liner notes: "Peter, Paul and Mary are not only three of the greatest folk artists ever, but also three of the performing arts' most outstanding champions of social justice and peace. They have lent their time and talents to the Civil Rights Movement, labor struggles, and countless campaigns for human rights for decades, and their compassion and commitment remain as strong as their extraordinary artistry." After Dr. Martin Luther King's death, in many ways Coretta Scott King became a

Above: The trio performs "Blowin' in the Wind" with Bobby Dylan and Stevie Wonder to celebrate the inaugural year of America's new national holiday, Martin Luther King Day.

Right: Peter with Coretta Scott King. The trio and Coretta would sometimes cross paths at demonstrations and benefits in the years after her husband's assassination in 1968. Coretta continued to carry the banner of her husband's efforts with dignity and great strength, and the affection between her and the trio remained strong through the years.

personal link for us to the ongoing struggle for equality of blacks in America. Whether it was at a demonstration at the United Nations, at benefits connected to the ongoing Civil Rights Movement, or sharing the stage in song with her at Ebenezer Baptist Church in Atlanta celebrating her husband's life and legacy, Coretta remained a true hero of what the trio felt were perhaps our finest moments as citizens of the United States.

In the spring of 1986, the Philippine Consul General Leovigildo A. Anolin in New York invited us to sing at the one-year anniversary celebration of the People's Revolution (also called the Bloodless Revolution) that had toppled the corrupt and cruel regime of Ferdinand Marcos, who had ruled the Philippines for twenty-one years. The invitation was extended to the trio because the Philippine nuns who had placed flowers in the muzzles of soldiers' guns and knelt in front of tanks to stop them did so while singing songs such as Pete Seeger's "Where Have All the Flowers Gone" and Bob Dylan's "Blowin' in the Wind" that they had learned from our records.

We told the consul general that we would be honored to accept the invitation. We wanted to do more, though, and the

The climax of the trip to the Philippines occurred at Edsa, the plaza where the Bloodless Revolution had come to a head. The trio appeared at this celebration of the return of democracy before a crowd of more than two million people, our largest audience in an almost five-decade career. We performed "Blowin' in the Wind," "No Easy Walk to Freedom," "If I Had a Hammer," and "Puff, the Magic Dragon." About 150 Philippine children performed a dance choreographed to "Puff" in full ballet costume. Later, Peter read eleven-year-old Emily Hockson's winning essay. Emily's parents had immigrated to the US from the Philippines because they did not want their daughter to grow up in what Emily characterized in her essay as "a land with no freedom." Compellingly, she wrote that, to her, the revolution meant that, now that Ferdinand Marcos was gone and democracy had been reinstated, she and her family could return to their native land.

Peter, Paul and Mary pose in Malacañang Palace with President Cory Aquino and Emily Hockson, the eleven-year-old Philippine-American winner of the Philippine Essay Contest on the occasion of the first anniversary celebration of the so-called "Bloodless Revolution" that ended Ferdinand Marcos's dictatorial reign.

consul general was therefore presented with an idea Peter had of mounting a nationwide essay contest in the US for children eleven and under called the Philippine Essay Contest. More than 100,000 students ultimately participated, writing on the topic, "What the Philippine Revolution Means to Me as an American." The response to this contest by the Philippine government could not have been more enthusiastic. We were told that President Cory Aquino personally requested that a responsive contest be mounted, asking her country's children to write poems and paint pictures on the same topic.

Senator George McGovern guest-hosts an episode of *Saturday Night Live*. The skit shown here was taped a month after his 1984 presidential campaign ended, and featured McGovern as president. Actors Joe Piscopo, Julia Louis-Dreyfus, and Brad Hall (left to right) played the trio.

Above: Peter, Paul and Mary perform at the 1987 American Music Awards. **Right:** The trio sings the National Anthem before game four of the 1987 World Series. As Mary described the performance in the *Bucks County Courier Times* the same year, "'The Star Spangled Banner' is not every singer's dream. First, it's hard to sing. It has a wide vocal range—an octave and a half—with one piercing high note. Devising parts becomes a three-part harmony nightmare. Also, singing in a ballpark is not a singer's dream of the perfect place to play. The reverberation of voice is such that whatever you just sang echoes back two seconds later, just as you begin to sing the next line. What was it like to sing the anthem at the World Series? Absolutely, unequivocally terrific."

There were actually three large marches on Washington for women's rights—not one, as some people believe. We performed as a trio at the first march on April 9, 1989, which was attended by more than a million people and, between the three of us, we maintained a presence at the marches in 1992 and 2004.

Mary was politically a feminist and a remarkable role model for young women. Her directness and the way she interacted with men, as well as the manner in which she stood her ground when being challenged with what she saw as an abuse of authority, was a study in fearlessness and courage. Mary was never a knee-jerk advocate for any social or political perspective. Instead, using the platform of her position in Peter, Paul and Mary, she was a leader: determined, thoughtful, and insightful. Mary was a maverick, especially among those who counseled a meek approach or the following of a party line that she felt spelled appeasement or a failure of nerve to confront an issue, an organization, or a person who was being unjust.

We were always at our best when we sang at demonstrations, benefits, and marches dedicated to matters of advocacy and conscience. Brief though our appearance was at this women's march (we only sang a couple of songs), for us it was thrilling and inspiring.

We stated our position on choice through a rewrite of the lyrics of an old union song, "Which Side Are You On?" Mary sang lead on this one, as only Mary could, and the crowd roared its approval. *I'm not pro-abortion. I'm pro-choice here today, and I'm protecting the Constitution of the USA. Which side are you on? Which side are you on? Which side are you on? Which side are you on?*

The unified spirit of hundreds of thousands of people marching for the rights of women in the 1990s and 2000s was strongly reminiscent of the 1963 Civil Rights March.

The trio met Nelson Mandela when we sang "No Easy Walk to Freedom" at an event honoring him in Tokyo, shortly after his release from prison. He told us that, at some time during his twenty-seven-year incarceration, when he was on Robben Island in South Africa, he'd actually heard Peter's song. Later, Peter encountered him at the celebration of President Clinton's inauguration. As Peter later wrote, "I proudly introduced President Mandela to my daughter, Bethany. Many years after she had demonstrated, and been arrested, with the trio in front of the South African embassy, Bethany made a documentary in South Africa called *Mama Awethu,* funded by a Yale undergraduate fellowship. The film told of the miraculous power of the poorest of black women who, with little more than their courage, their music, and their love for each other, paved the way for an apartheid-free South Africa. When he heard the story of Bethany's film, President Mandela embraced Bethany warmly, as did the women in his entourage. Needless to say, Bethany was deeply honored to meet one of her true heroes."

Above: Anti-apartheid leader and African National Congress (ANC) member Nelson Mandela raises a clenched fist as he arrives to address a mass rally several days after his release from prison in the conservative Afrikaner town of Bloemfontein in 1990.

Right: The title song of our 1986 album, *No Easy Walk to Freedom,* was written for Nelson Mandela.

The title of the song "No Easy Walk to Freedom" came from Mandela's famous quote: "There is no easy walk to freedom anywhere and many of us will have to pass through the valley of the shadow of death again and again before we reach the mountaintop of our desires."

No Easy Walk to Freedom

Brother Martin was walkin' with me,
and every step I heard liberty.
Tho' he's fallen, come a million behind!
Glory, Hallelujah, gonna make it this time!

Chorus:
No easy walk to freedom,
no easy walk to freedom.
Keep on walkin' and you shall be free.
That's how we're gonna make history.

[Chorus]

Across the ocean,
the blood's running warm.
I hear it coming, there's a thunderin' storm.
Just like we lived it,
you know that it's true,
Nelson Mandela, now we're walkin' with you!

[Chorus]

In our land, not so long ago,
we lived the struggle,
and that's how we know.
Slavery abolished, comin' freedom's call.
Keep on walking and Apartheid will fall!

[Chorus]

Bread for the body, there's got to be,
but a soul will die without liberty.
Pray for the day when the struggle is past.
Freedom for all! Free at last! Free at last!

[Chorus]

PETER, POLE + MARY

The trio's association with freedom struggles led to this absurd, yet somehow complimentary, postcard from the 1990s. The head of Lech Walesa, Poland's then-president and leader of the Solidarity Movement, replaced Noel's in a delightful play on words and switched faces.

In 1990, the trio performed at the twentieth anniversary of Earth Day in San Francisco. This was part of a series of worldwide events in more than 180 countries. To honor the year's focus on clean energy, the trio sang John and Johanna Hall's poetic and moving anthem of the 1970s' Anti-Nuke Movement, "The Power Song" ("Give Me the Warm Power of the Sun"), as well as "The Garden Song," written by David Mallet. The trio's growing support of the Environmental Movement became a rededication to the ecological concerns voiced by the trio some twenty years before at the 1978 Diablo Canyon/Survival Sunday anti-nuke demonstration. The seriousness of the environmental challenges we would soon face were not yet apparent to us or to the vast majority of Americans.

However, the seeds of today's huge and critical prioritization of doing all we can to turn back from our current path toward catastrophic climate change were sown in those early days. The leadership of Jackson Brown, Bonnie Raitt, and John Hall, great activists all, took us early to a place that is now an almost desperate grassroots struggle to literally save the planet.

As serious and dedicated as the trio was in regard to our activism, one of the most important aspects of our friendship, as well as our performances, was our shared enjoyment of each other and our ability to laugh with, and (lovingly) at, one another. Laughter became one of the great gifts of our relationship, as it frequently is in marriages and deep friendships. Early on, when Noel did his comedy, we would delight in his antics, watching from the wings. When he was onstage and "doing a bit" (on average once a performance) we'd break out into uncontrollable gales of laughter. Peter would be the first to lose it, Mary would follow, and then Noel, observing that we had totally broken character, would join us with unconcealed glee and appreciation.

Noel's humor included an uncanny ability to mimic all kinds of sounds, including machines, regional accents, cars, the wind, smacked golf balls, and explosions. One of his early stage bits involved duplicating the sound of the flush cycle of an old American Standard toilet, which caused Bob Dylan to refer to him as "the toilet man." Noel could characterize both the voice and mannerisms of people as varied as a snobby bigot in one moment and, the next, a spaced-out casualty of the

hippy era. He would precede some songs with improvised comedic sketches that were like short radio dramas—Julia Child in outer space or President Nixon on a skateboard—all wonderful and delightfully absurd.

Noel's humor became the foundation for many of the trio's comedic songs, which, right from the start, were always part of our concerts. Noel wrote many of these songs, such as the trio's hit "I Dig Rock & Roll Music" and an early classic, the charming "It's Raining, It's Pouring." Audiences also adored Noel's solo comedic songs, such as the one in which he unwittingly makes a spectacular outfield catch in the last verse of "Playing Right Field." Cheers always followed this tour de force, as if it had actually occurred in an onstage baseball game. Such was Noel's gift. Invariably, he'd take us all on what was a believable, yet improbable and hilarious, journey.

Left: Senator Ted Kennedy addresses supporters about a minimum wage increase in a park across from the US Capitol in 2005. **Above:** The trio with Ted Kennedy

In the early years, the majority of our social/political efforts were directed at grassroots campaigns such as the Civil Rights and Anti–Vietnam War Movements. Initially, like many other performers, we did not trust the world of politics because, inherently, politicians have to compromise to be effective. As young idealists, we had yet to learn that compromise can sometimes be an art form, other times an abandonment of principle, and sometimes a bit of both.

As we grew older, we began to recognize that, for our advocacies to become realities, those who sought change needed to acquire political power as well as people power. In 1984, we began working with our dear friend and organizing guru, Margie Tabankin. Margie had been a great student leader in the Anti-War Movement, was superbly skilled in grassroots organizing, had been the director of Vista (the domestic Peace Corps) during Jimmy Carter's presidency, and knew DC politics "cold." With Margie at the helm, we embarked on a series of about a dozen appearances for senatorial and congressional

DENNIS THE MENACE

"WE GAVE HIM A HAMMER. HE HAMMERS IN THE MORNING, HE HAMMERS IN THE EVENING ALL OVER THIS LAND!"

In the 2004 Iowa presidential primary, as in many of Kerry's past campaigns, Peter preceded the senator's appearance with rousing sing-alongs from the trio's repertoire. In Iowa, Peter also sang a campaign song he'd written for the senator, in this case, to an audience of firefighters and police from the town of Pleasant Hills.

candidates that became the prelude to our advocacies in the electoral political arena for the rest of our years together. Candidates we campaigned for included Senators Tom Harkin, George McGovern, Ted Kennedy, Eugene McCarthy, Max Cleland and Secretary of State John Kerry, all of whom would later become our friends, our heroes, and sometime allies.

Friendships with people in politics grew and, as time passed, we took pleasure in joining elected officials at informal events that celebrated their positions in government. Sometimes we raised money for them, and sometimes we sat around and shared some plain old fun. For instance, the trio visited with Dick Celeste, for whom we had campaigned in 1985, at the Governor's Mansion in Columbus, Ohio. After dinner, we relaxed in the living room, kids sprawled on the floor, telling stories and singing songs from the progressive song bag of years' past. It was a family gathering in the best of senses. In President Clinton's administration, we were invited to perform at the traditional White House egg-rolling contest, and spent some

The trio performs at Kent State University in 1995 as part of the twenty-fifth anniversary of the National Guard shootings that killed four students and wounded nine others. We embraced and prayed with the survivors, some in wheelchairs. We honored the slain students and pledged to "keep on keepin' on." In addition to a concert, we also participated in a teach-in, recalling the days when almost all the universities across America called for a complete moratorium on classes save for political organizing meetings focused on ending the Vietnam War.

delightful moments greeting the president and first lady. On another occasion, we made an after-concert visit to the Kennedy family compound following a summer performance at the Hyannis Melody Tent. Several generations of Kennedys shared post-concert laughter, more songs, and sweet reminiscences. Another time, we sang at the Special Olympics, an initiative very dear to Ethel Kennedy and now led by Tim Shriver. Later, there was the Sing-In for the Arts on the steps of the Capitol building, where Ted Kennedy's great booming voice dominated the twenty or so members of Congress who sang along. Such moments continued, and such precious friendships with elected officials and some of our grassroots' heroes endured over many years.

Above: The trio and President Bill Clinton at one of a number of campaign appearances we made for him
Right: The trio sings on the White House lawn during the annual Easter egg roll in 1993.

Above left: Phil Ramone, one of our most loved and respected recording career gurus, consults and advises Peter and Noel during the playback of a mix.
Above right: Noel and Ronnie Gilbert share friendship and laughter during the production of the PBS TV show *Lifelines*.

The family of folk—that is, performers who cut their teeth on traditional roots music and its more recent incarnation as music that touches hearts, stirs our conscience, and builds community—is a special group of people with special relationships. Together, we did what we could to walk-the-walk of the music's message. In the family of folk, there is little or no jealousy, rarely a sense of competition, and strong mutual support in times of personal trials. There is also trust, genuine love, and deep appreciation of each other as artists and as friends.

Some members of this folk family occupied special places in our artistic lives and in our hearts. The Weavers showed the whole folk family the way to live the message of the music, not just sing it. Particularly for those of us in the 1960s' Folk Renaissance generation, The Weavers were our heroes and our teachers, whether they knew it or not. Ronnie Gilbert was an idealistic, warm, wonderful friend. She was also a feminist well before the term was coined, and a source of inspiration for the trio, particularly Mary. We all fairly worshipped Odetta, crowned early on as the "queen of folk music." Her unique, startling voice could literally pin one to the wall with its power and passion.

Love and respect among folk singers also went out to the people who were part of creating our records. One such person who did not perform on our records, but who was nevertheless essential to our creative process, was a certifiable genius, Phil Ramone, an engineer, producer, and brother of kindred spirit. Similarly, we were all extremely appreciative of the

Left: Mary sings "House of the Rising Sun" in a blues duet with iconic folk singer and civil rights activist Odetta. **Middle:** Paul Prestopino, master of guitar, banjo, mandolin, and more, sits in his characteristically colorful overalls during the taping of *Lifelines*. **Right:** Dick Kniss, the trio's bass player and stalwart "fourth voice"

brilliant musicians who accompanied the trio and other folk artists, including back-up guitarist Bruce Langhorne, whose licks on our first albums are legendary; Paul Prestopino, the master of mandolin, banjo, guitar, and Dobro, whose knowledge of folk music and its styles was vast and of impeccable taste; and bassist Bill Lee (father of the renowned film director Spike Lee), who recorded our first four albums with us and who backed up virtually all the performers at the Newport Folk Festival.

In personal terms, superseding all others, for Peter, Paul and Mary, there was always an extra-special place in our lives and our hearts, personally and musically, for our beloved performing partner, bassist Dick Kniss. Dick joined us for all but a couple of the earliest years of our career. His background was jazz, and he was one of the most intuitive and adventurous players we ever encountered. Dick literally breathed the spirit of the music with us onstage. He sensed, perfectly, where a song was going on any particular night, and he always found new licks to challenge himself and us. Dick's contributions enhanced our voices, adding an extra level of surprise and improvisation to every concert we played with him.

In 1994, we assembled a group of wonderful folk singers to create a record produced by Phil Ramone, appropriately called *Lifelines*. Dave Van Ronk, Odetta, Richie Havens, Holly Near, Tom Paxton, and John Sebastian, as well as Pete Seeger, Ronnie Gilbert, and Fred Hellerman of The Weavers, all joined us. The CD and video present a proud picture of us united with some of our most beloved members in what we always considered to be our remarkable family of folk.

The call came in 1997 from Martha Hertzberg, our young and wonderfully capable manager who worked with the trio for twenty-eight years, first with our manager Ken Fritz, and then guiding the trio's career on her own from 1996 to the present. Martha was a partner in organizing many of our later social-political appearances and advocacies. A progressive in her own right as well as a PhD candidate in anthropology, Martha was a voice of passion and knowledgeable insight, bringing important causes to our attention and helping us to pursue them. When she shared details of the United Farm Workers' (UFW's) continuing plight and renewed efforts in the 1990s to organize migrant workers, in this case the strawberry pickers based in Watsonville, California, we heeded that call as we had for the UFW in the '60s during the Grape Pickers' Strike. Pesticides were causing widespread health problems, the fields lacked potable water and toilet facilities, and the vastly underpaid "stoop-labor" work was backbreaking. Martha interfaced with the head of the UFW, Arturo Rodriguez, the son-in-law of Cesar Chavez, to organize a benefit concert by the trio and a trip to the fields of Watsonville, CA. Our goal was to witness the facts on the ground and to increase public awareness of the urgent plight of the strawberry pickers. Efforts such as this, which called upon us to use our music in some way to advance a cause or advocacy, were a major factor in keeping the trio together through the proverbial thick and thin. Such efforts united us in ways that superseded the kinds of arguments and squabbles that, though only human and natural, can break up groups like ours when members become weary of dealing with such challenges.

When we visited Watsonville, we were struck by the brilliantly colored waving red flags and by the workers and their families who greeted us with explosions of gratitude. They cheered when we finished "If I Had a Hammer," Woody's song "Deportee" about migrant workers, and, of course, "Blowin' in the Wind." Seldom had an audience touched us so deeply. It was stirring, but also heartbreaking, to receive their dignified, open, grateful embrace. In some heart-to-heart exchanges with the United Farm Workers' leaders, we found out what you cannot know from the printed page or from secondhand descriptions: theirs was a struggle for survival under the constant shadow of illness, hunger, and possible death due to horrific working conditions, virtually no health services, and miserably low pay. They embraced us as brothers and sisters, and our hearts went out to them. In return, they gave us the gift of acceptance, as much for us simply showing up to

support them, as for our music. We returned from that trip refreshed and reenergized, ready to carry on the work and sing our songs with a clearer understanding of the challenges we faced.

Efforts to better the working conditions for strawberry pickers were largely successful. It was the legacy of Cesar Chavez, who changed the consciousness of America about some of our most forgotten and cruelly exploited workers. Woody Guthrie spoke of these workers in the lyrics of "Pastures of Plenty": "Pull beets from your ground, cut grapes from your vine, to set on your table that bright, sparkling wine." In Watsonville, we had come full circle from the '60s to the '90s. The struggle for fairness and justice for the poor was, is, and, alas, will continue to be ongoing.

At the trio's request, Bill Cosby came to host one of their New York Choral Society holiday concert celebrations at Carnegie Hall. This concert was also a benefit fund-raiser to launch the Save One Child Foundation.

In the early nineties, the trio was scheduled to perform the Holiday Celebration Concert at Carnegie Hall. Such concerts, performed every other year for about three decades, were benefits for the New York Choral Society, which featured 180 nonprofessional, but extremely gifted, voices. The society was directed by Robert DeCormier, the trio's beloved musical director after our reuniting in 1978. We all adored him, but he was a super-special friend of Mary's from her earliest years at Little Red, the elementary school where Robert once taught music. The trio would sometimes combine this benefit concert with a fund-raiser for yet another cause or nonprofit, and sometimes for a political candidate. In one instance, the Carnegie concert became a platform for launching Save One Child, a new foundation that would pay for individual children's medical treatments, transport them and their families to New York, and pay for all expenses including post-operative care in the US for as long as was needed.

The Holiday Celebration Concert was a great success and the foundation was born. Milton Glaser generously designed a beautiful invitation. Our dear friend from the Greenwich Village days, the extraordinarily gifted comedian, actor, educator, and advocate, Bill Cosby, agreed to MC the show. The spirit of that concert was memorable and Drs. Alex Berenstein and Fred Epstein were honored from the stage, as well as Michael Miller, head of the Toys "R" Us Children's Fund that paid for the benefit's expenses and the initial funding for Save One Child. As of now, more than two hundred children's lives have been saved through the efforts of Save One Child, which continues to inspire doctors and staff as it saves lives, one child at a time.

New York Choral Society and Peter, Paul and Mary's Music Director Robert DeCormier with Noel and Mary

Noel and graphic designer Milton Glaser share the delight of decades of projects together and the warmest of reminiscences about the trio's beginnings.

Over the years, Milt became our "go to" genius for all the design and graphic conceptual projects of the trio. We formed a lifelong friendship with Milt, who was one of the kindest, most generous, most perceptive and gifted people we ever met.

The photograph on our first album cover became an iconic image for the trio, and we still have vivid memories of the day of the photo shoot. We all assembled at The Bitter End coffeehouse on Bleecker Street in Greenwich Village, the site of our first paid engagement, and the set was a flurry of activity. The photographer, Bernard Cole, arranged the lights and chose the camera's position while Peter spoke with our managers, Albert Grossman and John Court. Offstage, someone arranged a bouquet of yellow roses and handed them to Mary. Just before we stepped in front of the camera, Milt stepped up to the brick wall background with several pieces of colored chalk in hand. With casual assuredness, he drew a *P*, another *P*, and an *M*; then he drew a heart around the initials.

The liner notes for the album were highly unusual and unlike what was ordinarily printed on record jackets of the time. The phrase "Honesty is back. Tell your neighbor," was written by John Court, Albert's management partner. These words helped to shape the way our audience saw us, and helped propel our first album to the top of the charts, where it lingered and "revisited" the Top 10 for the next three years.

Both Albert and John genuinely believed that there was a special quality of directness and honesty in our singing and in order to preserve that, in practical terms, they negotiated a recording contract that allowed us to limit record companies' prerogatives that quite likely would have asked us to change our musical style and dictated our choices of songs. Negotiating such a contract constituted a huge leap forward. Compared with the prerogatives that were previously afforded recording artists, this contract gave us and the other performers Albert and John represented the great gift of not having to compromise our musical taste, our message, or our social/political advocacies as expressed in our music. This was highly unusual at the time because, like movie companies that virtually "owned" actors, most record companies were intent on controlling as many aspects of the careers of their musical artists as possible. They dictated the material to be recorded and how it would be produced. They decided which tracks were acceptable, which had to be remixed or eliminated, as well as all the design elements of the album covers. In fact, when Peter, Paul and Mary first auditioned for a series of record companies, more than one made it clear that, although they were interested in signing us, for us to be on their label, we had to change our repertoire (!). Working under such commercial constraints would have meant eliminating some, or many, of the songs on our first album, the one that defined us as a group and on which we were allowed to make all our own musical choices.

The importance of Albert and John finding a small, fledgling record company housed in a Quonset hut on the back lot of Warner Bros.' film studio, called Warner Bros. Records, which later became a giant in the record industry, and negotiating a contract that gave us total creative control over all aspects of our records, cannot be overstated.

Warners' folks became our friends and allies, not just our business partners. They respected us, not just for our successes, but for our advocacies, as well. Warner Bros.' President Mo Ostin, our special buddy, and Mo's "mirror image" Joe Smith, and Don Graham, an amazing PR guy who broke our first single, were all super to us. Later, folks such as David Altschul, Kevin Gore, and Kris Ahrend picked up the baton. Such trust and friendship sustains even today, after more than fifty years. Few recording artists have ever been so fortunate.

Top: Peter receives a chiropractic bear hug from Noel, during the reception following the marriage of Martha Hertzberg, the group's manager. **Middle:** Noel and Mary share a laugh and an offstage moment of delight. **Bottom:** Mary dances with the bride.

Left: The trio and their bassist, Dick Kniss, join Pete Seeger at the 2003 tribute to Harold Leventhal at Carnegie Hall, New York. **Above:** Peter and Pete Seeger collaborate before recording the opening chords of "River of Jordan," the closing song on the trio's album *Lifelines*.

Carnegie Hall was the site of many performances by Peter, Paul and Mary. It was also the site of two historic concerts by The Weavers, one in 1955, a seminal and inspiring event that both Mary and Peter attended as teenagers. Forty-nine years later, in 2003, we performed at Carnegie Hall in a tribute concert to The Weavers' manager Harold Leventhal. We joined the original members of The Weavers onstage, save for Lee Hayes, who had sadly passed some years before. This 2004 concert harkened back to 1955 when The Weavers were blacklisted by the House Un-American Activities Committee (HUAC). Because of the blacklist, no club or other venue would hire them to perform; that destroyed their shooting-star career. Earlier that year, Pete had been brought up on charges before HUAC and convicted for refusing to answer, though the sentence was later reversed. In 1955, Harold Leventhal, a person of great principle and another of the trio's heroes, paid for the rental of the Carnegie concert hall out of his own pocket, taking a huge financial risk. Without this gesture, there would have been no other way for The Weavers to sing in this distinguished venue and the concert that launched legions of folk singers like Mary and Peter would never have taken place.

Above: Matthew Shepard's parents, Judy and Dennis, embrace the trio onstage.
Left: Audience members hold tiny flashlights aloft while singing "Light One Candle" at the Matthew Shepard concert of healing in Laramie, Wyoming.

In 1998, Matthew Shepard, a twenty-one-year-old senior at the University of Wyoming, was murdered by two young men in a viciously brutal, anti-gay hate crime that shocked the nation. The cause of this murder has recently been contested by some who assert that it was a drug-related crime. Notwithstanding, this horrific murder made America aware of the severity of homophobic hatred that had infected our society. At the behest of Matthew's college, Peter, Paul and Mary traveled to Laramie, Wyoming, for a town gathering to show support for Matthew's parents, and also to show solidarity against gay bashing and hate crimes directed at lesbians and gays across the US. Our concert, presented to almost the entire Laramie community, fell on the eve of the trial of the second of Matthew Shepard's killers, the first having been convicted months earlier.

At the concert, Mary sang "Home Is Where the Heart Is," a moving anthem about a lesbian couple's love for their child. Peter sang "There but for Fortune" with an added verse he wrote immediately after visiting the deeply rutted muddy field where Matthew was hung on a fence to die: "Show me a gay man, hated and scorned. Killed for just being, the way he was born. And I'll show you a young man, with so many reasons why. There but for fortune, go you or go I. You and I." We also sang "Light One Candle," during which the audience took the tiny flashlights that had been passed out when they entered and waved them over their heads in the way matches were once lifted in solidarity during the Civil Rights and Anti-War Movements. The performance was a vivid display of a community united against hate, and it had a powerful effect. At the end of the concert, Matthew's father, Dennis, said, in tears, "To tell you the truth, Peter, the healing just began tonight." Clearly, the outpouring of support from the community affected Matthew's parents, Dennis and Judy, very deeply.

Shortly after her successful bone marrow transplant, with resolute determination, Mary fulfills her goal of performing at PP&M's Carnegie Hall holiday concert. It was a highly emotional and joyous occasion.

In November of 2004, Mary received devastating health news: she had acute myelogenous leukemia (AML), a fast-growing cancer of the blood and bone marrow. Two rounds of chemotherapy at Danbury Hospital and Memorial Sloan-Kettering Cancer Center did not provide a cure, but she went on to have a successful bone marrow/stem cell transplant at Sloan-Kettering. Mary received more than ten thousand supportive e-mails (and she read every one) from concerned fans all over the world. "It was enveloping; it was like a big warm blanket," Mary said in a 2006 interview with *Connecticut Post* writer Eileen Fischer.

The trio continued performing for another four years—at Mary's insistence. Our first concert after the transplant was at Carnegie Hall with a full orchestra and the New York Choral Society, and the first four rows of the audience were filled with doctors and staff from both hospitals. Mary's physicians had found her donor through the National Marrow Donor Program. In gratitude, Mary committed herself to publicizing the organization and encouraging people to register their marrow, particularly on behalf of people of color for whom the odds of finding a match were much slimmer, due to far lower funding for the African-American population. She met her marrow donor, Mary DeWitt Hessen, before a concert at Ravinia, a large performing outdoor shed in Highland Park, Illinois. The wellspring of joy and gratitude that they shared was nothing short of magnificent. They were both named Mary, both had two daughters, but one Mary was a Republican and one was not, as our Mary pointed out hilariously at the concert. Of course, the bond they shared was far stronger than party affiliation, and lasted until Mary's passing more than four years after her successful bone marrow transplant.

Robert DeCormier conducts the orchestra and chorus at the trio's last benefit for the New York Choral Society.

During breaks between rehearsal times at Mary's apartment in early 1960, Peter and Noel could often be found at the Fat Black Pussycat cafe on MacDougal Street. Then, the Village scene was as much a state of mind as it was a geographic location. Many a spirited discussion of politics, philosophy, and poetry took place while contemplating a chess move, sipping a mug of hot cider at a coffeehouse, or shoulder to shoulder at the bar of the local "watering holes" with a writer, an artist, or possibly even one of The Clancy Brothers.

So, in 2007, when the editors of *Vanity Fair* magazine asked the renowned photographer Annie Leibovitz to create a picture portfolio of legacy and contemporary folk artists to appear in their November issue, she arranged for The White Horse Tavern to serve as the location for the trio's photo shoot. For Peter, Paul and Mary to receive an invitation to be included in this feature was both a compliment and a challenge. Although Mary had been cured of the leukemia, she was still somewhat fragile following the

Above, from left: Noel, John Mayer, Mary, Stevie Wonder, Whoopi Goldberg, and Peter at the annual Songwriters Hall of Fame Awards in 2006 **Below:** The trio celebrates receiving the Sammy Cahn Lifetime Achievement Award from the Songwriters Hall of Fame.

After almost fifty years, the trio returns to the White Horse Tavern, an iconic Greenwich Village hangout for songwriters and authors, for a *Vanity Fair* photo shoot with Annie Leibovitz.

radiation and the chemotherapy and then, of course, there was the hair . . .

Mary's chiseled cheeks and intense eyes, sometimes hidden, sometimes highlighted by her long straight hair and iconic bangs, were now softened, framed by a shorter, casual, tousled look. How would this subtlety translate to camera?

The answer is self-evident. Arguably one of the most compelling photos ever taken of the trio, Leibovitz managed to capture the warm, embracing, familiar nature of the old Village environ, the visual proof of Mary's newly reclaimed health, as well as the nuanced, loving relationship of three longtime friends.

There was a triumphant spirit in us when, at Mary's bidding, we continued to perform for almost four years after her victorious bout with cancer.

Above and left: The trio and our beloved "band," as Noel called Dick Kniss and Paul Prestopino, became extremely close during our last years performing together. Whether onstage or rehearsing, it was always a celebration with the sense that a farewell was not far off.

During her final two years, Mary performed in a wheelchair. She inhaled oxygen through nasal tubes and, to minimize the audience's concern, she called them her "new jewelry." We sat next to her in chairs so we would remain—literally and spiritually—on eye level with her.

Despite the inflammation in her lungs, which limited Mary's intake of air, Mary delivered some incredibly moving, powerful performances during our last concerts. We never knew how or from where she drew that vocal power, but she did, and the audience loved her all the more for her obviously heroic efforts.

Our petty considerations and fears slipped completely away during this time, and we cherished the times we could be together. In her final months, Mary handled her declining health in the bravest, most dignified, and generous way imaginable. She never complained. She avoided expressing her emotional and physical distress, trying not to worry those of us who loved her, especially her wonderfully attentive husband, Ethan. Mary hid whatever pain or fear she might have felt from everyone, clearly so as not to be a burden.

Proudly, Mary did not die of cancer. In fact, she was cancer-free at the time of her death. Although the chemotherapies had saved her life, they left her with lung inflammation that required steroids, which other organs in her body could not tolerate in the long term. We continued performing until four months before she passed on September 16, 2009.

Although we had campaigned for a number of presidential candidates and, in that context, had shared some fleeting exchanges with them, President Obama's personal letter to Mary wishing her well as she dealt with the challenges of cancer was a most significant gesture.

His presidency was the fulfillment of a dream of Mary's, of ours as a trio, and of so many in our country who had dared to hope that, one day, the nation would take this giant step forward.

At the inauguration, one could palpably sense the unbridled elation, wonderment, and pride of those assembled as we stood in a crowd that was estimated to be more than seven times larger (District of Columbia's official estimate is 1.8 million) than the quarter of a million who assembled for the 1963 March on Washington. As in 1963, you felt that no matter whom you approached with a request such as "Gimme a hug," black, white, brown, anyone who was there, they'd reply, "Sure," and oblige with a big proud grin, affirming the magnitude of the achievement we were there to celebrate.

As Peter recalled, "The two of us from the trio had come to experience the moment and savor the victory, of course, but also, in a way, to share it with Mary. She was in our hearts when we saw this new history being made. She deserved to be there. In a way, we held Mary's proxy so we could share it as a trio."

THE WHITE HOUSE

WASHINGTON

June 30, 2009

Ms. Mary Travers
Apartment 5FE
27 West 76th Street
New York, New York 10023

Dear Mary:

I recently learned about the challenges you face, and I want you to know how much I admire your strength. My thoughts are with you, your family, and friends as you continue your brave battle.

Your passion for music and your ability to stir change has helped define a genre and a generation. I hope you take special pride in all of your accomplishments, as they are rich and many.

In the days ahead, please know that you will be in my prayers.

Sincerely,

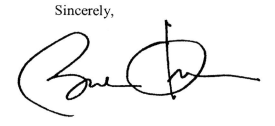

Above: An enormous crowd gathers to celebrate the inauguration of President Barack Obama in 2009. Noel and Peter attended with memories of the 1963 Civil Rights March on Washington, gratitude and amazement at the nation's progress, and with Mary in their hearts. **Right top:** Peter and Noel onstage with Ben Vereen at an inaugural ball **Right bottom:** Noel, Peter, and Noel's wife, Betty, celebrate with Nancy Pelosi and her family.

There was a moment onstage in the early 1960s when, as we were performing "If I Had a Hammer," Peter and Noel realized that, as Mary was singing the song, she had also become really angry. After we got offstage she explained that, while singing "Hammer," she'd looked out at the audience of students at Ole Miss where James Meredith had courageously desegregated the school. It had been a bastion of entrenched racism, but Meredith successfully desegregated it after winning a lawsuit that went all the way to the Supreme Court. While singing, all of a sudden she realized that, although the audience was singing along and cheering our "hit," they were really cheering for the idea of, as she put it, "the hammer of justice and the bell of freedom for whites only"—which made her livid. That was Mary: someone who believed that every moment we were onstage had to be a moment of truth—truth to be shared, truth revealed so that we never lied to ourselves, to each other, or to those for whom we sang. With Mary, the chips had to fall where they were. That's part of what made her so special.

Over the course of our fifty-year life together, Mary's favorite parting phrase was ". . . to be continued." It was her way of recognizing our never-ending examination of the balance between personal life, song, and activism . . . of resuming a dialogue that grew from a provocative question . . . of returning to the lingering laughter of a joke or the threads of a conversation the next time we came together.

Mary's phrase ". . . to be continued" took on a different meaning after her passing in the fall of 2009. On those occasions when Peter and Noel perform together today, there are certain songs that resurrect her in spirit. Her voice, her tossed hair, those jangling bracelets on her right arm jabbing and punctuating a lyric with an angular and vital delivery—sometimes and somehow the absence of Mary is felt as powerfully as her presence once was.

Perhaps this will be ultimately true of us all. It's not the number but rather the quality of the moments we share that are truly remembered. And, maybe the most meaningful message we leave behind is ultimately not the specifics of the cause, the date of the rally, or the number of people in attendance. Maybe it's about recognizing the spirit of goodness in us all . . . the caring for the least of us . . . and the work that is to be continued . . .

PETER YARROW

Above: Peter and Eliezer Adoram, Peter's first professional singing partner, in the Aviv Theatre of Dance and Song, 1959 **Top right:** Multitasking in 1962. **Bottom right:** Peter's earliest love, painting, 1962

Opposite page, left: Peter and Mary Beth McCarthy, married in 1969 **Opposite page, top right:** Peter and daughter Bethany at the Kerrville Folk Festival **Opposite page, bottom right:** Peter and son Christopher at home in Trancas Beach, California, 1974

Above: Peter hugs granddaughter, Bethany's daughter, Valentina, age six. **Left:** Christopher, Bethany, and Peter during an annual visit to the Kerrville Folk Festival in Texas in the early 1990s

Opposite page: Peter sings at a rally for Soviet Jewry in Milwaukee, Wisconsin, 1987.

Personal life for me combines the joy and wonderment of a life partner; an unimaginable infatuation with my two children, and now a grandchild; and my solo work as a performer, the vast majority of which springs from the same commitments to justice and peace that were the focus of Peter, Paul & Mary's advocacies. That these appearances for causes, benefits, and demonstrations can now be shared with one or both of my children is a source of delight and pride beyond compare. It is hard to imagine a greater privilege than performing with these two wonderful, caring, passionate, and talented human beings, Christopher and Bethany (whose partner, Rufus, is a brilliant iconoclastic cellist who also joins the Yarrow clan onstage). The love and respect we share, and the commonality of belief in a shared ethic, shines within us when we perform together and gives me a sense of completion in a way that I never knew would be possible.

I am blessed to have shared a beautiful marriage with Mary Beth McCarthy, with whom I fell in love during the presidential campaign of her uncle, Senator Eugene McCarthy. Our hearts were bound in a love born in that amazing late '60's era of hope, determination, and idealism, and we loved each other in ways that reflected the passion of those halcyon days. Though we are no longer together as romantic life partners, we are best friends, and what we share as co-parents and grandparents is, in many ways, as good as it gets.

I remain what some would call a workaholic, but not really. I can be a fiercely dedicated party person and I love to lay back, ski, and veg. Alas, my passion for painting and the plastic arts is seldom pursued, though I long for a sabbatical when I can ignore the persistent beckoning of *Tikkun Olam* (a Jewish phrase meaning healing the world) and indulge myself in the visual arts and go back to school. (How I long to be nourished, once again, in that way.)

NOEL PAUL STOOKEY

Above: Noel's high school rhythm and blues group, The Birds of Paradise, performs live on Ed McKenzie's Saturday morning television program in 1955 during an on-air competition against four previous winners. Noel's group won first place. **Left:** Noel at Michigan State University during his sophomore year, 1957

I moved to Michigan when I was eleven years old. Skinny, gawky and an only child, music helped me to find my voice (pun intended) in that new community. The Birds of Paradise, my six-member rhythm and blues group, became a social touchstone in our high school. After three years at Michigan State University, I moved to New York City without hesitation, filled with the self-confidence that Midwestern acceptance and encouragement uniquely provides. Whether as a salesman or cameraman, photography had

Above left: The newlywed Stookeys returning to Betty's parents' house for the wedding reception in September of 1963 **Above right:** Noel and Betty in Boston in 1960

always provided me with employment, and within a year I was working on Fourteenth Street as the production manager for a photographic chemical company during the day, and playing chess in Greenwich Village by night.

In 1959, I ran into a high school friend, Betty Bannard, while exiting a Seventh Avenue subway. At the time, neither of us knew the other was living in the city, or that we had found our soul mates. Four years later, we were married, and in 1965 we celebrated the arrival of our first daughter, Elizabeth.

As the trio's touring, performance, and recording schedule expanded, maintaining family life in cozy, historic Greenwich Village became increasingly difficult. Searching for a personal peace and stability that would ultimately lead to renewing my Christian faith, Betty and I made the life-changing decision to move our family (now augmented by the birth of our twins, Anna and Kate) to the coast of Maine.

Above: Daughters Kate, Anna, and Elizabeth on a family trip to Australia in the late 1970s
Right: Summer visits from extended family have been known to encourage unpredictable behavior! In this photo, we may have refrained from donning red rubber noses, but we weren't content with normal portraiture, either. Back row, left to right: Daughter Anna and husband Greg Corbin, daughter Liz and husband Paul Sunde, John Boit, and (seated) daughter Kate with grandson Oliver. Betty and I are seated, behind grandsons (left to right) Finnian and MacIntyre Sunde.

In 1994, Betty began studies at Harvard Divinity School. After graduation, she was appointed Chaplain at the Northfield Mount Hermon School in western Connecticut. I became artist-in-residence at the school, teaching classes and producing events on campus, including a benefit concert by the trio.

Our home in Maine has become Camp Stookey. While holidays tend to be reflective and sedate, the summers are much different. Our daughters bring their families, and the grandchildren take golf, tennis, and sailing lessons in between multi-generational soccer games on the back lawn. The kitchen is filled with a joyous cacophony of "many hands with pots and pans" prepping family meals and debating whether dinner knives should be set blade in or blade out. No small wonder that when someone calls for a family photo, we respond enthusiastically!

Above: Noel and his Greenwich Village "roommate," Tom Paxton
Top: Noel and his Grammy-nominated Bodyworks band. Members included Denny Bouchard, Karla Thibodeau, Alan Diaz, Kent Palmer, and Jimmy Nalls.
Left: Meeting Prime Minister Shinzō Abe in 2007

Just as the song "El Salvador" had encouraged the trio to observe firsthand the political landscape of Central America in the late '80s, "Song for Megumi" brought me to Tokyo. I wrote the song as an appeal for the release of a thirteen-year-old Japanese girl abducted by the North Korean government. While in Japan, I met with Prime Minister Shinzō Abe and made several television appearances.

To sing folk music is, ultimately, to live its ethic. And, whether in the context of my family, Peter, Paul and Mary, the Bodyworks band, or my long and abiding respect for my friends and fellow folkies, I am continually amazed and thankful for all of the coincidences that continue to make up my life.

MARY TRAVERS

"Since I was a young girl, I found great solace and peace in horses. My first encounter with this huge, beautiful beast captivated me. I'd watch them prance and be delighted when they let me ride (and horses do let you ride them at their pleasure)."

Above: Horses were one of Mary's passions, and she often spoke of the sense of freedom she felt with them during her early years. This photograph was taken when she was in her mid-twenties.
Left: Mary singing with friends from Elizabeth Erwin High School

Above: Mary and younger daughter Alicia **Left:** Mary and daughters Alicia, then age three (far left), and Erika, then age ten (far right), along with beloved cat Sam at home in Redding, Connecticut. Alicia still calls this image "the dirty feet photo."

"Children remind us that love is simpler than adults make it. That life is full of beauty and some of it fills us with awe."

"I come from a small family and have always thought of my closest female friends as sisters . . . part of my family, and they made me feel like a part of their families."

"We are four generations of women learning from each other. Perhaps the most important thing I've learned is just how lucky I am."

Top right: Mary and husband Ethan having fun in the pool **Bottom right:** Mary and four generations of women: her mother, Virginia; children, Erika and Alicia; and grandchildren, Virginia and Wylly **Top left, top middle, and lower left:** Mary enjoys time with friends Shelley Dowell (top left), Maddy Miller (top middle), and Shelley Belusar (lower left), her friend and tour manager since 1971. Mary's circle of female friends was a great source of support and love to her.

"Being a grandparent is not an intellectual job. It's purely visceral. It feels good. They love you; you love them."

"But now you know that since your child has learned to survive, so will hers. Now you have a sense of your own mortality; your immortality is mirrored in your grandchild's smile. And somehow that softens the fact that you have a limited time here."

"Dogs are ten percent fur and ninety percent love."

Above: Mary with her beloved dog, Peaches
Right: Mary and the love of her life, husband Ethan Robbins. Ethan says this photo captures the oneness of their relationship.

"One of my great personal accomplishments was to have a real 'Press Card.' I had been writing for a great daily newspaper in Bucks County and my editor gave me a press card. I loved it . . . it looked so official. Here's the kicker: Ethan and I went to an art show in Manhattan and we couldn't get in . . . sold-out audience.

"'I'm sorry,' the young woman at the ticket booth sweetly explained, 'It's sold out . . . all the admissions that are left are for the press . . . ' I showed her the card . . . and in we went."

INDEX

IMAGE CREDITS & ACKNOWLEDGMENTS

Image Credits

Front cover: Fred W. McDarrah/ Contributor/Premium Archive Collection/Getty Images

Back cover: © Annie Leibovitz/ Contact Press Images

Spine: Michael Ochs Archives/ Stringer/Michael Ochs Archives Collection/Getty Images

Page 11: Michael Ochs Archives/ Stringer/Michael Ochs Archives Collection/Getty Images

Page 12: © John Byrne Cooke (left)

Page 12: Michael Ochs Archives/ Stringer/Michael Ochs Archives Collection/Getty Images (right)

Page 14: Michael Ochs Archives/ Stringer/Michael Ochs Archives Collection/Getty Images

Page 15: Shel Silverstein (left)

Page 16: Archival material from the December 1965 issue of Playboy magazine. Reprinted with permission. All rights reserved.

Page 17: Warner Bros./Hulton Archive Collection/Getty Images

Page 18: Barry Feinstein (left and right)

Page 19: The Estate of David Gahr/ Premium Archive Collection/ Getty Images (top left)

Page 19: The Estate of David Gahr/ Premium Archive Collection/ Getty Images (top right)

Page 19: The Estate of David Gahr/ Premium Archive Collection/ Getty Images (bottom)

Page 20: © Jan Dalman

Page 21: © Jan Dalman

Page 22: Barry Feinstein

Page 23: Barry Feinstein

Page 25: Hulton Archive/Hulton Archive Collection/Getty Images

Page 28: © Bernard Cole Archive

Page 29: Barry Feinstein

Page 30: © Bernard Cole Archive (right)

Page 31: Fairfax Syndication

Page 32: ©1967 Jan Dalman (left)

Page 32: Bob Gomel /Contributor/ The LIFE Images Collection/Getty Images (top right)

Page 32: Jon Brenneis/Contributor/ The LIFE Images Collection/Getty Images (bottom)

Page 33: © Bernard Cole Archive

Page 34: AFP/AFP Collection/Getty Images (top)

Pages 36-37: Fred W. McDarrah/ Contributor/Premium Archive Collection/Getty Images

Page 38: © Richard Voges

Page 39: © Richard Voges

Page 40: Michael Ochs Archives/ Michael Ochs Archives Collection/Getty Images

Page 42: © Lisa Law/Lisa Law Productions (top left)

Page 42: Express Newspapers/ Hulton Archive Collection/Getty Images (top right)

Page 42: © Robert Corwin (bottom right)

Page 44: From the collection of Mary Katherine Aldin

Page 45: AP Photo

Page 46: © Mirrorpix

Page 50: Douglas R. Gilbert/ Contributor/Redferns Collection/ Getty Images (top)

Page 50: © Joe Alper Photo Collection LLC 2012 by Joe Alper (middle)

Page 50: The Estate of David Gahr/ Premium Archive Collection/ Getty Images (bottom)

Page 51: © Jim Marshall Photography LLC

Page 52: © John Byrne Cooke

Page 53: © John Byrne Cooke

Page 55: Pictorial Parade/Archive Photos Collection/Getty Images

Page 56: AFP/AFP Collection/Getty Images

Page 57: William Lovelace/Hulton Archive Collection/Getty Images (right)

Page 61: Pictorial Parade/Archive Photos Collection/Getty Images

Page 62: NBC/NBC Universal Collection/Getty Images (top)

Page 62: NBC/NBC Universal Collection/Getty Images (bottom)

Page 63: Folk Music, 1967, Zen-on Music Co., Ltd. (left)

Page 63: Barry Feinstein (top and bottom right)

Page 64: © Nicholas Zurek

Page 66: © Ken Regan/Camera5

Page 67: © Ken Regan /Camera5

Page 68: © Meyer Liebowitz/The New York Times

Page 69: From "MAD Follies" #2 © 1964 E.C. Publications, Inc. Used with Permission. (top)

Page 70: Library of Congress Prints and Photographs

Page 71: Archive Photos/Stringer/ Archive Photos Collection/Getty Images

Page 72: Fred W. McDarrah/ Premium Archive Collection/ Getty Images (right)

Page 73: © Paul Davis

Page 76: AP Photo/Ray Stubblebine (top)

Page 76: © Ken Regan/Camera5 (bottom)

Page 77: © Ken Regan/Camera5

Page 78: © Peter H. Rosen/Visionary Artists Resources Including Other Unique Services (V.A.R.I.O.U.S. Media)

Page 79: © Peter H. Rosen/Visionary Artists Resources Including Other Unique Services (V.A.R.I.O.U.S. Media)

Page 80: © Scott Goldsmith

Page 81: © Karin Epstein

Page 82: © Robert Corwin (top)

Page 83: © 2013 ThomWolkePhotography.com

Page 84: © Deborah Raymond (top left)

Page 84: © Marilynne Herbert (top middle and top right)

Page 84: Designed by Milton Glaser (bottom left)

Page 85: © Marilynne Herbert

Page 87: © Susan Meiselas/ Magnum Photos

Page 88: © Cynthia Johnson/The LIFE Images Collection/Getty Images (top)

Page 89: © Cynthia Johnson/The LIFE Images Collection/Getty Images

Page 90: © Robert Corwin (top)

Page 90: © Sally Farr (bottom)

Page 91: © Robert Corwin

Page 92: AP Photo (left)

Page 92: © Steve Ziffer (right)

Page 93: © Manolet Agoncillo and Ang Pathayagong Maloya (right)

Page 94: NBC/NBC Universal Collection/Getty Images

Page 95: Ron Galella/Ron Galella Collection/Getty Images (left)

Page 95: Focus On Sport/Focus On Sport Collection/Getty Images (right)

Page 96: © Robert Corwin

Page 97: © Robert Corwin

Page 98: © Martha Hertzberg (left)

Page 98: Cynthia Johnson/ Contributor/The LIFE Images Collection/Time & Life Pictures/ Getty Images (right)

Page 99: © Gunnar Johnson (right)

Page 100: © Lisa Law/Lisa Law Productions

Page 101: © Lisa Law/Lisa Law Productions

Page 102: © Robert Corwin (right)

Page 103: © Robert Corwin (top right)

Page 104: Win McNamee/Staffs/ Getty Images News Collection/ Getty Images (left)

Page 105: © DENNIS THE MENACE © 1993, North American Synd. (left)

Page 105: AP Photo/Laura Rauch (left)

Page 106: © Jeff Glidden

Page 107: © Thomas John Gibbons (top)

Page 108: © Robert Corwin

Page 109: © Robert Corwin (left)

Page 109: © Sally Farr (middle and right)

Page 110: Jeff Greenberg/ Photolibrary Collection/Getty Images

Page 114: © Robert Corwin

Page 115: Don Addis/Tampa Bay Times (top)

Page 115: © Robert Corwin (bottom)

Page 117: © Martha Hertzberg (top)

Page 117: © Robert Corwin (middle)

Page 117: © George Carranza (bottom)

Page 118: © Robert Corwin

Page 119: © Marlene Carstens/UW Photo Service

Page 120: © Robert Corwin

Page 121: © Robert Corwin

Page 122: L. Busacca/WireImage Collection/Getty Images (top)

Page 122: Ryan Born/WireImage Collection/Getty Images (bottom)

Page 123: © Annie Leibovitz/ Contact Press Images

Page 124: © Robert Corwin

Page 125: © Robert Corwin

Page 127: © Martha Hertzberg

Page 129: © Sylvia Plachy

Page 130: Barry Feinstein (top and bottom right)

Page 132: © Maryte Kavaliauskas (right)

Page 133: © Linda Schwam Merkel

Page 137: AFP/AFP Collection/ Getty Images (left)

Page 138: Barry Feinstein (right)

Page 139: Photo © Maddy Miller/ Maddy Miller photo.com

Page 140: Photo © Maddy Miller/ Maddy Miller photo.com (top middle)

Page 140: Photo © Maddy Miller/ Maddy Miller photo.com (bottom right)

Page 141: © Robert Corwin (right)

Acknowledgments and Thanks

Designer: Maria Villar

Editor: Dawn Cusick

Mary Katherine Aldin, Tony Arancio, Beth Bradford, Allan Braun, Jim Brisson, Raymond Collins/ Illinois State Library, Lisa Glines, Meredith Hale, Rachel Jackson, Peter Laird, Ethan Robbins, Alex Shulman, and Alicia Travers.

Special thanks are extended to Robert Corwin, our unofficial and beloved photographer over PP&M's entire career.

Special thanks go out to Mike Renshaw, Mary's long-time editor and the editor of her book, A Woman's Words, who researched Mary's writings and guided us to many of the special quotes used in this book.

Peter, Paul and Mary's Record Company: Warner Bros. Records and Rhino Records

Peter, Paul and Mary Management: Martha Hertzberg, Walkstreet Management, Venice, CA